Class, Language and Education: Class Struggle and Sociolinguistics in an African Situation

by
H.E. Newsum

Department of Black Studies

The Ohio State University
Columbus, Ohio

Africa World Press, Inc.

P.O. Box 1892
Trenton, New Jersey 08607

Africa World Press, Inc.
P.O. Box 1892
Trenton, N.J. 08607

Typeset by TypeHouse of Pennington, Inc.

Cover design by Ife Nii Owoo

Library of Congress Catalog Card Number: 89-81017

ISBN: 0-86543-139-6   Cloth
        0-86543-140-X   Paper

To
Okpara and Chinyere

For
SFC and Walter

Acknowledgement

Thanks to my friends in Socialist Forum Collective (SFC) and the Department of English Language at the University of Ife. Special thanks to Geof Hunt, Segun Osoba, Lekan Oyeleye, Niyi Oladeji, Bisi Afolayan, and Wanda Macon.

Contents

Symbols

| | | -   **sentence boundary**

  | | -   **clause boundary**

    | -   **phrase or group boundary**

   // - **(enclose) specimen of phonological transcription**

   / - **foot boundary**

Preface

The following discussion was originally presented in the Department of English Language at the University of Ife in Nigeria in June of 1981. The present work covers both the first and second half of the original work, although some portions which appear in the earlier work have been omitted, and new pieces added. The second half of the original discussion, as with the present addresses the role of language capital in the Nigerian educational system and its appropriation vis-a-vis the general Nigerian population. The present, however goes into greater detail on the question of value although neither the earlier discussion nor the present do justice to this complex phenomenon. This latter half goes on to show the role played by the English language in the formation of the Nigerian class structure.

Because most audiences, unsympathetic to Marxism, prematurely judge African and Third World Marxist theorists and revolutionary activists (among other independent Marxists), and wrongly assume them to be proxies of Soviet chauvinism, the discussion of this paper caused some discomfort and paranoia among some members of the Ife audience who derailed the question and answer period of the first seminar. Unfortunately, this seminar became a shouting match with rightists and agnostics on one side and leftists on the other. Befitting the paper, the Ife audience comprised scholars from all arms of the humanities and social sciences. In spite of all the brutal attacks and counter-attacks, the first seminar enjoyed a wide variety of opinions from different academic angles.

Since so many people (including those who prefer witch-hunting to science) are misinformed about the theoretical thread of Marxist thought—and this was indeed evident in the first seminar—we have attempted to go into some detail about a Marxist perspective on class stratification and social consciousness which may appear to be boring and unnecessary. This aspect of the discussion is not isolated to the

V

present work; we assume this as a continuous responsibility given the state of general awareness about Marxism, even among the erudite communities.

H. Ike Okafor-Newsum

Introduction

The premise of this discussion holds that social class and social consciousness are determined by the production relationships in a society and that language in the social context of capitalism, where a hostile and dialectical interrelationship between class groups exists, reflects the social (class) character of participants and the nature of their interactions. This, however, to some of us is obvious. This business of the social stratification of language is usually explained in terms of class roles with elaborated language at one end of the spectrum and restricted language at the other. The two codes are consequences of unequal accessibility to the desired cultural capital (Bernstein, P. 103 also see Bourdieu) of a bourgeois class system. Manufacturers of these concepts associate, in a grandiose way, abstract thinking and the linguistic self-sufficiency of the message to users of "elaborated" codes (i.e., the educated and well-to-do-class), and cognitive poverty to users of "restricted" codes (i.e., the underclass, the downtrodden). These precepts are the products of a kind of sociolinguistics that is loaded with a bourgeois bias that supports the social and material foundation of the present division of labor. In this case, or moreover in the contemporary world, language, specifically at the meta-level (above the common place) of the code scale, and Western education, as a supposedly midwife of social change in a bourgeois democratic society, are manifestations of surplus capital and are symbolic representations of the ideological (*superstructure*) and material base (*infrastructure, stuttura*) of the class system and therefore, constitute forms of cultural capital. Status quo language and Western education are cultural compulsives* necessary for acceptance into the high life of the bourgeoisie. In the context of this paper, cultural capital and cultural compulsives are one in the same. In a class system, the acquisition of cultural capital is more often than

---

*See Harold Cruse, *The Crisis of the Negro Intellectual*, pp. 53 and 60-63. Cruse explains V.F. Calverton's concept of "cultural compulsives." These are established cultural values and phenomena required for success in a society or organism of it.

not a privilege governed by a tendency to limit access, and although bourgeois democratic legislation and its judiciary theoretically thwart this tendency, elite class objectives foster the de facto form. Along with the basic fact that profits and consumer markets are more important to capitalists than a government-guaranteed provision of basic communal needs, this tendency to limit access is no doubt one of the factors contributing to the competitive nature of the capitalist class system.

Language educationalists in Western countries have addressed the question of elaborated and restricted codes by offering theoretical explanations, descriptions and pedagogical approaches to it, often with the view of remedying the problem of restricted codes as manifested in school children. Though from an educational point of view the contributions of language educationalists are admirable and worthwhile, they are nonetheless (with a few exceptions) politically shallow. Western education is hardly a pedagogy of the oppressed, although it may foster the ideal of egalitarianism. Historically, Western education is certainly not an enemy of a capitalist class system, about which we are concerned. At best it is an apology for capitalist exploitation. The premise of this discussion holds that the determining factors of accessibility or the non-accessibility of cultural capital, that is, the production forces and the collective conscience of society, must be radically changed before any assurance can be given to resolving the question of dialectically related codes.

Although the question of dialectics will always permeate nature and society, the nature of dialectical relationships in human interaction is always subject to social, political, and economic determinants. It is the collective social, political, and economic will of people which decides the nature of human dialectics.

In this discussion we will attempt to discuss some historico-political and economic factors relevant to the capitalist class system which impinge upon the social character and meaning of language (for the most part with reference to the sociolinguistic situation of Nigeria). Throughout this discussion we shall concern ourselves with the following: 1. social class and class consciousness; 2. social consciousness as a governing agent of language, and language as ideologue; 3. class consciousness and class roles as reflected in language (dialogue and anti-dialogue); 4. the politics of cross-cultural and cross-class scholarship; and 5. the bourgeoisie as a sociolinguistic entity and its relationship to capital and the appropriation of surplus.

It can be argued that our descriptions and explanations of social classes, class consciousness, and the connected character traits of class groups are not without exceptions. For these exceptions, wherever they may exist (and we do acknowledge such exceptions), we will offer no explanation; rather we shall focus only on the examples presented in our discussion.

In a multilingual, multicultural and multinational society like Nigeria (a peripheral "capitalist" state)*, which also faces the legacy of forced bilingualism and biculturalism of which English and Western life style constitute imposed systems lending to the double consciousness of modernized Nigerians and the prevailing class system, an approach is needed to social development that initiates nation-building from the bottom (of the society) up, that is, from the peasant-proletariat vantage point to the highest prevailing socioeconomic formation. In this light there needs to be a new orientation toward the appropriation of the surplus of production. This we admit to be idealist philosophy. When we speak of social development from the bottom. . .up, we are expressing a primary concern for a development plan that embraces the sociocultural, sociopolitical and socioeconomic realities of the masses, first and foremost. Within this viewpoint the sociolinguistic terrain of Nigeria and the role which English (the educated variety and pidgin "English") has played in the history of that society does not go unnoticed.

It is hoped that this discussion will be of value to social scientists, sociolinguists, political activists and members of the broad intellectual community who are concerned with revolutionary praxis.

---

*Our reference to Nigeria as a peripheral "capitalist" state needs some clarification. Nigeria is, in historical and material reality, *a dependent-neo-colonial-consumer state* governed by the whims of a renegade contractor-comprador sector aspiring toward capitalism in a society which has not cultivated an ethos for such an industrialized mode of production. Nevertheless, we shall use the term, "capitalist," when referring to Nigeria only on the basis of the warped aspirations of the elite class—not on the exclusive basis of historical and material considerations.

What is Class?
(an introduction)

The historical relationship between nature and human necessity has influenced societies generally. Yet beyond this, "the improvement in organization of work from being an individualistic activity towards being an activity which assumes a social character through the participation of many," (Rodney, p. 11), has shaped man's relationship with mankind. The manner in which work is organized, along with the sociological and material basis for its organization, and the manner in which people benefit from their collective productivity is actually at the core of the class question. "Slaveowners and slaves were the first important class divisions." (Lenin, *The State*, p. 8) Societies are stratified on the basis of labor participation and prestige. The latter here can be based upon mere symbolic criteria with limited ownership of capital.

Since the bourgeoisie (artisans turned industrialists) assumed greater power over the traditional aristocracy, and since the ownership and control of productive forces have become the determining factors of social control, the monopolization of the productive forces and of raw materials necessary for industrial growth determines power relationships.

Even in contemporary times, the democratization of capital has not changed the power relationship. For example, as Lenin observed of the democratization of the ownership of shares in Western Europe in the twentieth century before the Second World War:

> experience shows that it is sufficient to own 40 percent of the shares of a company in order to direct its affairs, since a certain number of small, scattered shareholders find it impossible, in practice, to attend general meetings, etc. The democratization of the ownership shares, from which the bourgeois sophists and opportunists so-called 'Social Democrats' expect (or say that they expect) the democratization of capital, the strengthening of the role and significance of small scale production, etc., is in fact, one of the

ways of increasing the power of the financial oligarchy. (*Imperialism, The Highest Stage of Capitalism*, pp. 54-4)

The denominations, which Lenin goes on to explain, have changed over several decades; however, our basic observation about the power relationship in the capitalist class system has not. What should be noted, however, is that the big shareholders (the real owners) are monopoly capitalists who possess greater capital power, and the democratization of share-owning has, in fact, bolstered the power of monopolists. Though material in nature, the individual shares of small shareholders are only of symbolic importance in the final analysis. Their capital value is too small to constitute much material significance or to wield any effective power over production objectives. The owners of small shares are at best petit and/or petty bourgeois*. This sector of the capitalist class system is reformist and, in fact, has no objective interest in revolutionary change.

Now that in the process of explaining "power relationship" in a democratic capitalist system we have exposed sections of the bourgeoisie, let us continue explaining social class formations in some detail.

Social history provides us with descriptions of class formations. There are the preordained rulers, the aristocracy, a rather precapitalist caste who are nowadays absorbed into the bourgeois superstructure in some countries; the bourgeoisie, big artisans turned big industrialists, who own and control production and control the flow of capital (this includes the agricultural bourgeoisie); the petit and/or petty bourgeoisie who are small merchants, small artisans, spiritual leaders, doctors, jurists, bureaucrats, military agents, academicians - or in a capsule, those who nowadays own capital but wield no power over production; the proletariat, (an advent of industrialization, also in modern agriculture) who are middle income and small wage earners, and who are more often than not less educated than the bourgeoisie (a foreman represents the affluent of this class); the peasantry (farmers), who are usually destitute small landowners of tenants; and finally the lumpen-

---

*In the Western world, bourgeoisified proletariats (the non-professional middle-class product of mass culture) are among this group.

proletariat, whose subsistence cannot be clearly determined. Amongst these categories of stratification, somewhere along the scale with wage earners, peasants and the lumpen are the unemployed. While in more experienced and older capitalist states this sector relies on welfarist institutions for subsistence, in the urban areas of underdeveloped capitalist countries this group would fall under the category of lumpenproletariat.

Marx's description of class formation is contained in what many scholars consider to be his definition of class. In *Capital*, Vol. III, Marx says:

> The owners merely of labour-power, owners of capital, and landowners, whose respective sources of income are wages, profits, and groundrent, in other words, wage-labourers, capitalist and landowners, constitute the three big classes of modern society based upon the capitalist mode of production. (Progress Publishers, p. 885)

Class as a conceptualization of reality is a complex phenomenon, and Marx's definition may be far too sketchy. But in simple terms we understand it to be the different stratified social groups in a society, each having a social, political and especially economic position (even in symbolic terms) in relations to the means of production.

Although scholars, even those belonging to Marxist schools, have not reached a precise agreement about what class is because of varying social situations in the world, there are meaningful contributions to the theoretical and practical application of the concept. (See Shivji, pp. 4-6)

Divisiveness within societies accommodates the ideological and material objectives of the mode of production, and the hierarchical structure of the class system where there is an exploiting class and an exploited class. Divisiveness serves the rulership (or the exploiters) by impeding the development of unity among the exploited and preventing the formation of a revolutionary class. These divisions in societies are along religious, sexual, chronological, territorial, ethnic, linguistic, racial, and educational lines, and have sociopolitical significance. These factors can (and do) influence an individual's relationship to the forces of production, even to the extent of determining whether a member of society can actually sell his or her labor, which is today a basic necessity for subsistence. This is what contemporary Marxists refer to as over determinism.

In the multiethnic and multiracial environments of the United States, the Caribbean and South Africa, for example, the defacto and dejure (the latter with reference to South Africa), manipulation of societal divisions helps draw the line between those who are eligible to benefit from the available surplus of production and those who are not, based upon ethnic and/or racial criterion. In terms of religion, the Muslim Turks during the heyday of the Sultans' rule oppressed Christian Greeks, and under this condition religion helped draw the line between capital (material and symbolic) and labor.

Divisiveness explains the formation of nationalist movements which are in constant competition. History shows that within such movements, there are desperate opportunists who constitute a petit and/or petty bourgeois class and are agents (collaborators) of the powers that be.

Divisiveness also plays a role in the social and moral consciousness of societies. There are fostered notions of superiority and inferiority on the basis of ethnicity, color* and religion (to name a few), or a combination of such criteria.

We shall offer one last example and explanation of divisiveness, which many intellectuals distinguish from the previous examples; this is the caste system. Though we have come to understand that under bourgeois democracy lower classes supposedly enjoy opportunities of upward mobility, there are extreme situations such as the "Brahman Caste System" in India, where lower "classes," castes, have no opportunities of upward mobility (at least before co-optation by colonialism). Individuals living under this system inherit pre-determined status which is constant from generation to generation.

Holding that a man's caste is right from the beginning, one must necessarily conclude that it is futile to rail at its limitations and

---

*It might be useful to point out that in our view race was not the basis of Western slavery. However, in the Americas, for example, the politics of color, "racism," that is, institutional racism is a consequence of the enslavement of Africans by Europeans. Nevertheless the initial motive of this epoch was the call for an appropriate labor force.

barriers. In fact, the individual who becomes dissatisfied with his status is pitted against his own caste. He will have to assume that he has been given a deal less just than that of his fellows; or that, while they merit their particular state, he deserves some rung above them. The gravity of such a position makes its occurrence practically inconceivable. (Cox, p. 42)

In Africa, in Nigeria to be specific, the phenomenon of caste stratification can be seen in the relationship between the "osu" (traditionally slaves) and the larger Igbo community. The osu system derives from traditional Igbo religion. The word "osu" means outcast. "Having been dedicated to a god, the osu was taboo and was not allowed to mix with the freeborn in any way." (Achebe, p. 192) The osu system has both a spiritual and material significance. Within the spiritual worldview of the Igbos the subjects of the osu system appeased the gods by serving them. But a subject of the system need not be a religious symbol. Until the coming of the abolitionist missionaries those Igbos captured, sold and/or bought as slaves were the predominant osus and constituted the labor force of the affluent.

The missions which settled in the area around Owerri (eastern Nigeria), which was heavily populated by osus, built churches, schools and colleges, which facilitated the social mobility of osus among the general population. While today's descendents of osus enjoy participation in politics, commerce and in some other aspects of mainstream social life, and have developed an impressive educated and affluent class, the possibility of them marrying a non-osu is virtually nil. And to this extent the caste system remains in operation.

Like in other situations of divisiveness, caste status determines the relationship of individuals to production and surplus capital. Let us not deceive ourselves; as implied earlier, there are traces (de facto and dejure) of quasi-caste stratification in bourgeois democratic societies.

In the modern world and in present Nigeria, the formation of social classes is not as cut and dried as the *owners of labor-power, owners of capital, and landowners.* Even in Marx's time, these classifications would not be adequate. However, we know that the more accessibility one has to the means and control of production in a capitalist state, the more power one wields. Though we know that in Nigeria there are individuals of preordained status (aristocrats), and though we know that top military officers have had their day, those who through "hook or crook" manipulate capital as big traders and big contractors (compradors) and big plantation owners constitute the major groups closest to the means of production. In other words these elements represent groups closest to the imperialist forces which actually own and control industrial production and finance. Compradors and plantation owners are major groups because of their capital power and because of their potential to expand and monopolize the economic base. Nevertheless, they are not the only engineers of social control in Nigeria; there are others who belong to the domestic superstructure as well.

In Nigeria, as in the larger world community, Western education or literacy is the most important social factor (cultural capital) determining one's nearness to or distance from the forces which govern societal affairs. As there are indeed hostilities between those who own capital and those whose labor can be bought and dispensed with (in a capitalist class system), there are condescending and defiant attitudes between those who are educated (among these are marginally significant capital owners) and those who are less educated (labor) respectively. The fact is that these groups are dialectically interrelated. It is through this dialectical relationship that the social consciousness of class groups and the corollary class struggle are made objective realities. It is this dialectic that determines lifestyle with all its intricacy.

Although no description of Nigeria's class formation can be totally accurate (in spite of the fact that its class stratification is more polarized than in more experienced capitalist states, and its elites are more autocratic), let us examine the following map of Nigeria's class structure.

A cline* exists between the extreme poles of the exploiters and the exploited. It is impossible to tell exactly where one category merges into the other, although one end is quite different from the other (in "binary opposition"). (Berry, Vol. I, p. 26)

---

*Although we find this concept useful for sociological purposes, Berry's pronouncement of the concept is purely of linguistic concern.

'MAP' OF NEOCOLONIAL CLASS STRUCTURE
(schematic & non-dynamic)

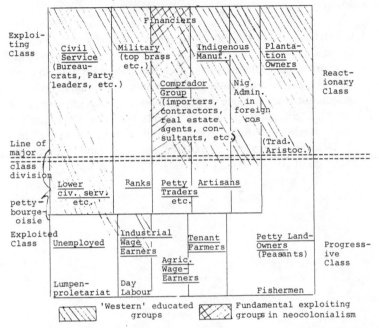

Before moving on, it might be useful to explain something about the exploiting group diagramed on the class map. It would be wrong to consider the big capital owners of Nigeria a proper bourgeoisie since they have no primary industrial base and are dependent on foreign industry and finance. Nonetheless, on the basis of capital power, in latter parts of this discussion we shall apply the term.

The exploiting class groups (see "exploiters" on the map) and the exploited are dialectically related to one another and have competing interests. *Though the exploited groups are not at most times consciously united, they are, as a political entity, competing for state power now in the hands of the exploiters.* State power in this respect is a combination of the informing economic base and the institutions of the civil superstructure, that is, the owners of, or in the case of Nigeria, those who have access to the means of production, and substantially benefit from its surplus and engineer the political and economic philosophy of the society.

I. Shivji in his book *Class Struggle in Tanzania* says that:
Lenin's profound observation that politics is a concentrated expression of economics conveys the important fact that the various class contradictions find their most mature and condensed expression in the struggle for state power. As Marx observed (said Lenin):. . .the political state represents the table of contents of man's practical conflicts. Thus the political state within the limits of its form, expresses. . .(from the political standpoint) all the social conflicts, needs and interests.* (Shivji, p. 8)

---

*"History shows that the state as a special apparatus for coercing people arose only wherever and whenever there appeared a division of society into classes, that is, a division into groups of people some of whom are permanently in a position to appropriate the labour of others, where some people exploit others." Lenin, *The State*, pp. 7-8.

Social Consciousness
and Colonial Ideologue
in Retrospect

Our discussion of the above sub-topic will be brief, and, therefore, we suggest that our readers review the works of Nkrumah, Mazrui, Moore, Hegel, and Engels listed in the bibliography of this work.

The Christian missions of the 19th century and early 20th century were not alone in giving morality to the epoch of European imperialism. The Western erudite community by virtue of its ideologue, that is its concern for genetic theory* and civilization building, also contributed to the moral justification of Western imperialism and colonialism without much concern for monotheism or divinity. The role which the ideologue of nineteenth century Euro-scholarship played in the shaping of social consciousness during that time and even in the contemporary period is worthy of our consideration. Nkrumah's *Consciencism* and Mazrui's *World Culture and the Black Experience* (to name only two) support this belief.

We cannot say that 19th century genetic theory is a product of Westerm imperialist objectives or vice-versa. What is true, however, is that genetic theory embraces the capitalist stage and industrial revolution and indeed considers them to be of a higher order of social development. Thus it can be said that leading European scholars—Charles Darwin, Lewis Morgan, George Hegel, George van Mauer, Frederick Engels, et al—all shared the view that Africa, in the 1800s, was still in the lower stages of development (savagery and barbarism),

---

*Genetic theory refers to the study of origin and development, that is, cultural development vis-à-vis material development. Such scholarship is also concerned with the role of biological gene structure vis-à-vis cultural and material development and this in fact has been a primary emphasis, though over exaggerated.

and yet financiers and industrialists of that same period looked to Africa, as they did to other parts of the non-European world, for markets and raw materials. Perhaps, to some extent, genetic theory and Western imperialism grew up together and indeed influenced one another and also arrested the social consciousness of Europeans and later their colonized subjects.

The genetic arrogance of super races before the 18th and 19th centuries rendered the world permeable to the cultural superiority disposition of Eurocentrism. In this respect Joshua Fishman (1960) says that:

> The association between a peoples individuality and its language is certainly an ancient one in the history of Western and Near Eastern civilizations. The ancient Greeks applied the term 'barbarian' (those who say baba, i.e., speak an incomprehensible tongue) to those to whom the gods had denied the gift of Greek, and the ancient Hebrews believed that their language was a uniquely holy vehicle that was created even before the world was brought into being and awarded to them as a particular gift of God. Certainly, linguistic specialness and in the inherent untranslatability of one's own vernacular or some other superposed language have been frequent components of the ethnocentrism and the worldviews of many peoples, past and present. (In Dasen and Berry, p. 64)

Thus, it is no wonder that in the past two centuries, and to an extent even in the present period, whenever an African acquires a European language and becomes a competent and sophisticated user of it, he proves to the European (all whites) the African's potential to be human. In this light, humanity is predicated not on language, but rather on European languages.

There is no better example of this kind of ethnocentrism than that of foreign language requirements in Western universities.

The grandeur given to the development of Western civilization and Western capitalism and industry, and the parallel notion of African savagery and barbarism, gave impetus to Western ethnocentrism (or Eurocentrism) and the arrogant and autocratic disposition of European civilizing missions in Africa. There was no African history before

Europeans took interest in the continent, and Africans who came in contact with missionary education and those who were later educated in Europe accepted this as correct. Nowhere in the history of Western colonialism is the language of the colonizer so impressive as in the works of the foundation demigods of genetic theory from Plato to Engels.

As a matter of consciousness building, it is unfortunate that many African students belonging to the first batch of Africans who received formal training at the beginning of the 20th century, read Western genetic philosophy with single-minded devotion. Some had already been singled out by missionaries and influenced by Western religious beliefs, consumer patterns, educational institutions and other elements derived from the culture of the colonial rulers. Because these colonial students were intellectually and, in some ways, also physically detached from their traditional roots, they were vulnerable subjects of the alien devices encountered in the Western erudite community. It is our guess (and Nkrumah has alluded to this) that this batch of colonial students, with a possible few exceptions, who received higher training and who became leaders in their homelands, saw no relationship between the causes of human problems, as presented by Western erudites, and the problem of being colonial subjects themselves. The more they internalized the language of the Western intellectual masters, the more they internalized the colonizers' autocratic authority and arrogance, even to the point of assuming Western culture (in the form of structural dependence) and supporting the weight of Western civilization on their shoulders. This is an aspect of hegemony.

In the long run, genetic theory as a most decisive element of colonial ideologue, inculcated self-rejection in the minds of the colonized subjects of Western imperialism, particularly in the minds of educated Africans in the early 20th century (not to mention the few who preceded them). After all, according to Western genetic theory, nothing was superior to Western development under capitalism, and this notion was even popularized among the colonized masses— *"Oyinbo" (European) things are always superior.*

As a final note to this juncture of the discussion we might consider that after all said by Darwin, Hegel, Mauer, Morgan, and a whole list of others, including Marx (using Engels as his agent), who were seminal influences in 19th century genetic theory, and given the material conditions* of that time, it is not surprising that the socialist, Frederick Engels who also dabbled in genetic theory, would endorse the French colonization of Algeria and claim that "the conquest of Algeria is an important and fortunate fact for the progress of civilization"** (notwithstanding his concern for exposing the contradictions of such an epoch with the view of realizing the socialist alternative). (Engels quoted by Carlos Moore, p. 18 - parenthesis mine.)

---

*The most important among these conditions are the growing interest in industrial advancements resulting from the invention of new machinery, the expansion of the capitalist market resulting from inflation and a high rate of production requiring a vast new consumer sector and raw materials, and finally the slow decline and eventual abandonment of slave labor in the Western world.

**For full text see Frederick Engels, "French Rule in Algeria," *The Northern Star*, January 22, 1848 (Quoted in: Karl Marx *On Colonialism and Modernization*, Edited by S. Avineri, New York: Doubleday and Co., 1968, p. 43.)

Language and the Class War
(dialogics and antidialogue)

One of the important characteristics in a portrait of exploiting class groups is the sociological and psychological phenomenon of sociocultural supremacy. This means that high social status is not just a measure of individual capital power but is as well a condition of the mind and life style; in other words, it is a measure of cultural capital, i.e., education and the mastery of metalanguages. How functionally relative one's labor is to the decision-making process of the societal superstructure and the industrial base in a capitalist mode of production is determined by the possession of specialized cultural capital. The more specialized and the more functionally-related one's labor vis-à-vis the machinery of social and economic control, the more socially "alienated", arrogant, condescending and powerful one is in relation to those whose lives are adversely affected by the prevailing social institutions and industry.

At the lower rungs of the social ladder, at the sub-structural level (among the exploited) we find a situation under which the masses of people are politically alienated. That is, while the exploiting groups have alienated themselves from the masses by concentrating power among themselves (in their own interest), the exploited masses are victims of alienation from the reins of power. The economic poverty of the lower-class groups has its own cultural face and, as J. Klein has inferred, there is "cognitive poverty" in a culture determined by economic poverty and the limited access to metalanguages. Klein also asserts that there is a "stubborn determination not to develop" on the part of the lower classes. Her specific reference here is to "a disinclination to develop the power to express oneself."* (quoted by J.B. Pride, p. 12) We consider this to be a rather myopic viewpoint. A

---

*This "disinclination to develop the power to express oneself" needs to be examined within the large complexity of class consciousness, not in isolation. It is also a positive act to resist the ascending culture.

careful observation of the collective psyche of lower-class groups (industrial and agricultural wage earners, tenant farmers, peasants, the unemployed and the lumpen), reveals that they, however courageous, have been systematically injected with fear, inferiority complexes, and powerlessness. The most tragic thing about members of the lower-class groups is that they have been so infused with the values of the prevailing superstructure, particularly those which are unscrupulously Darwinian, they are even enemies of themselves.

The collective psyche at the extreme ends of the social ladder constitutes the dialectically interrelated social consciousness of the exploiting groups and the exploited, respectively. Social consciousness is the psychological product (a reaction so to speak) of a concrete social material situation. Our concern in this essay is with linguistic reactions to the socioeconomic situation of a class system. Out of necessity one would form a certain attitude toward existence if confined to solitary darkness; the conditions of day-to-day reality form and conform our personal and collective psyche on the same principle. Depending upon where one is positioned in the social and economic terrain of society, one forms particular attitudes about oneself and others within one's socioeconomic camp and those outside it.

Social consciousness, at either end of the social ladder, is an informing agent of language. (We take into account the fact that the cultivation of language during and beyond the formative years does not simply take place by chance.) Language is formed in accordance with the social order and is subjected to the domineering institutions of social programming and control. Keeping this in mind, we consider that if the politico-economic philosophy and the production relationships of the society give rise to dialectically interrelated social classes, then it follows that a dialectic in the sociology of language will also exist. This is a sociocultural, sociolinguistic and socioeconomic consideration which grows out of the assumption that at the extreme ends of the social ladder there is a culture, complete with dietary habits, an intelligible system of communication, peculiar structures of family life, standards of education and health care, etc. determined by production and the manner of distribution of cultural capital. To exemplify the dialectic in the sociology of language in Nigeria, the class war between lower-class speakers of pidgin—not to mention those who are bound (restricted) to their mother-tongues—on the one hand and the fluent speakers of the prestigious varieties of English in the upper-class groups on the other, illustrates a sociolinguistic dialectic—a dichotomy of a colonial turned neo-colonial class system—where English is an imperial and second language.

Similarly, in an L1 (first language) situation, such as the United States, there is a rift between standard English (educated English) on the one hand, and on the other, so-called subdialects of English, particularly as spoken by African Americans, Appalachian whites, and Hispanic Americans to name just a few who constitute the lower working class.*

As best we can, and according to the available ethnographies and cross-class studies, we will now try to describe the extreme poles of opposed but interrelated sociolinguistic groups and the nature of their relationships in a class system.

Communicative (speech) situations, in which there is intragroup activity, in the well-educated middle and upper-class groups produce verbally explicit and boundless languages. This commonly accepted view does, however, ring of bourgeois bias. The upper-class groups have a significant degree of mastery of elaborated codes of sophistication, prestige, and control. But in addition to the mastering of elaborated codes, the upper-class groups may dabble in and out of restricted and elaborated codes (code switching), since they have the facilities to use both. Educated users may endeavor to code switch depending upon the level of familiarity with and degree of liberalism towards members active in a situation. This is a diaglossic consideration. (At any rate, there is room for compromise within the class.)

---

*Over the last two decades the question of nonstandard English dialects has permeated the citadels of English language and linguistic scholarship in the United States. In the specific case of African American speech, the same blackness that had rendered African Americans invisible before the 1960s became their trademark and the so-called "Black English" became the concern of language educationalists from all sides—from the pro-Black English of Geneva Smitherman to the cries of Johnny can't read—Johnny can't write—Johnny can't speak of the conservative golden agers. For those sections of the society which are bound to "nonstandard" dialects, this issue is not merely linguistic, it is cultural, political and socioeconomic.

Lower-class groups have little proficiency in the use of elaborated codes at the level of meta-talk and are bound to a "group oriented" and "consensus seeking" "nonstandard" variety of the desired standard usage. (The previous quotation marks are intended to suggest caution.)* Because of the relationship of working class people to the means of production and the nature of their labor in a capitalist class system, an elaborated use of language is usually not present among them, although a restricted use is unacceptable to the prevailing superculture which is supported by the philosophical and institutional objectives of the capitalist mode of production. Since the lower classes do not equally share with the upper classes the surplus value (money and cultural capital) of monopoly capitalism, there is little reason why they would or could have equal language capital with them. According to the conventional view, the language of the lower class is verbally "implicit" and relies on paralinguistic and extraverbal variables (on the one hand, prosodic elements, i.e., rhythm, stress, and pitch, and on the other, gestures and facial expressions, respectively). (See J.B. Pride, p. 13) Lower-class language is restricted in terms of vocabulary and syntactical variations.

Jerome Bruner provides a description of class differences in the use of language—minus the politics. The now well-known 1960s studies of educationists like Bernstein (1961), Hess and Shipman (1965) and Bee, et al. (1969)**, each concerned with the cognitive development and language of middle and lower class children, provide the empirical

---

*It is perhaps conceivable that status quo standard language is also group oriented, that is to say that standard varieties are by sociopolitical design confined to privileged class groups. "...In these days of extreme specialization everyone's knowledge is restricted." Thus all languages appear to be consensus seeking regardless of class. The academic jargons are extremely confined. This is a factor of voluntary alienation. (Also see "decontextualization" in the section of this essay entitled Pidgins, "Nonstandards" and the Politics of Cross-cultural and Cross-class Scholarship.)

**Basil Bernstein (1961), "Social Class and Linguistic Development: A Theory of Social Learning," *Education, Economy, and Society* ed. A. H. Halsey et al, New York: Free Press. Robert Hess and Virginia Shipman (1965), "Early Experience and Socialization of Cognitive Modes in Children," *Child Development* No. 36 pp. 869-886. Helen Bee et al. (1969), "Social Class Differences in Maternal Teaching Strategies and Speech Patterns," *Developmental Psychology* Vol. 1, No. 6 pp. 726-734.

background to this description in Bruner's essay "Language and Poverty":

> Two trends . . . seem to be operative in the *use* of language by middle class children. One is the use of language as an instrument of analysis - and - synthesis in problem solving, wherein the analytic power of language aids in reorganizing and synthesizing the features thus abstracted. The second trend is toward decontextualization, toward learning to use language (or using it) without dependence upon shared precepts or actions, with sole reliance on the linguistic self-sufficiency of the message. Decontextualization permits information to be conceived as independent of the speaker's vantage point; it permits communications with those who do not share one's daily experience or actions, and in fact does, as Bernstein (1970) insists, allows one to transcend restrictions of locale and affiliation. (*The Relevance of Education*, p. 149)

Of the lower class Bruner says:

> Lower-class language, in contrast, is more affective and metaphoric than formal or analytic in its use, more given to narrative than to causal or generic form. It is more tied to place and affiliation, serving the interests of concrete familiarity rather than generality, more tied to finding than to seeking. (Ibid. 149-150)

According to Bruner, the characteristics of lower-class language are not as they are because the lower classes are victims of the system (though he agrees they are). "It is rather that a set of values, a way of goal seeking, a way of dealing with means and ends become associated with poverty." (Ibid, p. 150) A whole movement for the "nonstandard" language of the lower class (see particularly works of William Labov) was launched to prove its logic, articulate its history, and argue that the literature of standard languages has had only irregular and scattered influence on spoken lower-class varieties. And yet discussions of this kind have only become more philosophical and more linguistically descriptive without dealing with the material poverty of the lower class (in its spatial text) or attacking the essential material causes of it in ideological terms or on a level of praxis. It is amazing to any true socially committed, but naive person, how the radical fortitude of such concern can slice through the pages of two decades, and when faced by the stubborn corporate demands for communicative competence, by-pass the revolutionary path only to drift toward the remote corners of the intellectual cosmos.

As already implied, the social stratification of language is the result of uneven distribution of cultural capital, i.e., metalanguages, and an institutionally programmed manner of goal striving. It seems more desirable to evenly distribute the cultural compulsives which we believe to be vital for good character building. Certainly we do not mean to suggest that everyone should be equally exposed to the varieties (registers) of sophistication merely so that the whole population can become doctors, lawyers, academics, managers and directors; certification in any of these professions does not mean that one has developed the self to the maximum potential, although in a bourgeois class system, one would have an economic advantage by doing so. To determine the state of self-development there ought to be proper ideological criteria determined by the goodwill of the collective conscience of the society at large. Development of human capacities must involve sharpening the dialectical awareness and critical abilities of women and men so that they can be self-determining. All laborers, regardless of their function, have the right to build upon their personal character, to continue the human metamorphosis (at the expense of those who benefit greatest from their labor, i.e.,government and industry) for the betterment of themselves as well as for the good of the whole social environment. The only time the capitalist, who regards labor as a mere commodity, is interested in building the character of any member of the labor force is when he wants to exploit his labor or influence for some specialized and extraordinary purpose. (In the more experienced and older capitalist states, such philanthropy is done in elaborate style, and where private enterprise is concerned, serves the purpose of qualifying for tax exemptions.)

In the work place and in the consumer market, compradors, petty bourgeois elements, and workers have daily contact. The first two classes involved in this interaction possess language as a form of cultural capital (as an asset), while the third class is restricted to a small portion of the cultural capital, and therefore cultivates a language of poverty, of restricted speech patterns, and of deficient reading and writing skills. Extremists who prefer emotionalism to science associate restricted codes or "nonstandard" varieties, exclusively and interchangeably, with "social deviants" and "cultural degenerates."

Intergroup activities between members of opposed sociolinguistic and socioeconomic realities produce a language which reflects the class roles of persons acting in the situation and sometimes there is noticeable condescension on the part of the upper class participants and defiance or passiveness on the part of lower class participants. This, however, and proceeding points in this section will be further examined later in the discussion.

The consciousness of exploiting groups and the consciousness of exploited groups respectively are in constant opposition—each group advancing the collective cause of the two respective divisions. The encounters of these dialectically interrelated psyches have dialogical ramifications. When explaining the dehumanization of dialogue, Paulo Freire provides a descriptive definition of dialogics:

Dialogue is the encounter between men [people] mediated by the world, in order to name the world. Hence, dialogue cannot occur between those who want to name the world and those who do not want this naming - between those who deny other men the right to speak their word and those whose right to speak has been denied them. Those who have been denied their primordial right to speak their word must first reclaim this right and prevent the continuation of this dehumanizing aggression. (Freire, p. 61)

The antagonism grounded in the linguistic interchange described above is (as Freire might put it) a "united reflection" of the dialoguer's circumstances; or, in other words, a dialogical reflection of people needing to define the world from different vantage points as a result of circumstances. The inegalitarian character of the dialoguer's relationship reflects a lack of mutual respect and mutual being. Under such conditions, the verbal interchange between the participants ceases to be dialogue and becomes antidialogue. Antidialogue is a dehumanizing activity: if it is in speaking their word that people transform the world by naming it, dialogue presents itself as the way in which people achieve significance as human beings. *True dialogue* requires positive mutuality. But antidialogue allegedly fosters a culture of silence among those who are not allowed to speak their word.

Further to our explanation of dialogics and antidialogue and to our broader discussion of language, a linguistic explanation of what is actually the social and communicative nature of language is necessary. Such a linguistic explanation should at least recognize the relationship of sociocultural and socioeconomic class roles to social consciousness (or vice-versa) and the connection between these two variables and the character of language. In other words, we are speaking of a materialist linguistics:

> Materialist linguistics must proceed from the principle of the integral connection between the social and communicative nature of language which is ultimately determined by the social character of human consciousness. The problem of the subjective and individual character of language (speech) may be solved, in the long run, only on the basis of the social functioning of consciousness of any member of the social group. (V. Yartseva, et al., p. 6)

If we accept that the problem of language can only be solved on the basis of the social functioning of consciousness, then we must also recognize the basis upon which social consciousness is formed, that is, the mode of production which is ultimately responsible for most of the social and psychological characteristics of societal members. Social consciousness is not inherently automatic; it is acquired in the historical, political and economic process of socialization within groups and as a result of interaction between groups. Throughout life, language reinforces the self-concepts of individuals and their perceptions of others within a multifaceted social order determined by the peculiar social character, history, and politics of economic productivity. M.A.K. Halliday, one of the seminal influences in systemic linguistics, in his book *Language and Social Semiotic*, says that language is:

> ... the linguistic interchange with the group that determines the status of the individual and shapes them as persons. (p. 14) In other words, instead of looking at the group as a derivation from and extension of the biologically endowed mental power of the individual, we explain the nature of the individual, as a derivation

from and extension of his participation in the group. Instead of starting inside the organism and looking outwards, we can adopt a Durkheimian perspective and start from outside the organism in order to look inwards. (Ibid)

This is our understanding of how language takes part in the replication of the group. Halliday's concern is for the individual in the group, but in addition to this concern we go further to say that groups (classes) do not reproduce themselves in isolation from opposing groups. What is essentially important to Halliday is that, " . . . language is the medium through which a human being becomes a personality, in consequence of his membership of society and his occupancy of social roles." (Ibid, p. 15)

From this point we shall deal with the social and linguistic intercourse of dialectically interrelated groups, each having a particular relationship to the means of production and the appropriated surplus, and a language reflective of that relationship.* Our concern here is for societies in general and Nigeria in particular.

The imperialist bourgeoisie, the big companies and subsidiaries of the British, Americans, West Germans, Japanese, French and their Western allies constitute the *transit superclass* in Nigeria, as well as all of Africa, Asia, and Latin America. In Nigeria, East Indians, Lebanese, Syrians and more so the larger indigenous comprador bourgeoisie provide the necessary link for imperialist domination as a whole. (These compradors are owners of import-export houses, big contractors, cocoa plantation owners, professional consultancy firms, etc.) The state functionaries and the intellectual engineers (custodians), that is, the Nigerian petit and/or petty bourgeois members of the state bureaucracy (this would include military bureaucrats), erudites and reactionary social activists, manage and protect the affairs of the state in the economic interest of the imperialist who in turn (directly and indirectly) takes care of the economic interest of the national compradors in the first instance and of the custodial elements of the society in the second.

---

*The ensuing social-politico-economic analysis borrows from Shivji's model of class formation in Tanzania, pp. 44-54.

At all levels, members of the big business sector, bureaucrats and professionals, meet the indigenous (marginally literate and illiterate in English) peasants, workers, unemployed citizens and small retailers in an antagonistic production relationship determined by the interest of the imperialist bourgeoisie and the domination of the national commercial sector by the Asian and indigenous compradors. It is through such contact that language inherits its social character. In situations of interclass activity, language functions as a reinforcer of individual social roles and ultimately collective class consciousness. Again as Halliday puts it, "language is the medium through which a human being becomes a personality," (loc. cit) and this process is continuous throughout life and permeates the collective psyche.

Although concrete day-to-day activities provide the best examples of how language reflects the dialogics of class consciousness and the self-concepts of speakers and receivers of dialectical socioeconomic status, literature as a mirror of life (though sometimes blurred by individual percepts) provides examples from which we can draw our illustrations. Our sample of "dialogue" or antidialogue, which is taken from an unpublished play, "The Beehive" by Uko Atai, depicts the Nigerian neocolonial situation in the individual and collective sociocultural personality of Nigerians, which is derived from a history of autocratic and authoritarian rule under colonialism and the present-day mode of production*. The linguistic systems of characters in the play are standard English and pidgin. Although our linguistic limitations do not permit us to borrow samples from the day-to-day use of indigenous languages or the mother-tongue literatures of the Nigerian people, we believe that in these languages, like in any others, we can find class differences. It is more than probable that, in the past and still now, there is a significant difference in the communicative competence of mother-tongue speakers living in the traditional metropolis or control centers (i.e., Benin City, Oyo, Ife, etc.) which host the citadels of political and cultural activity, and their counterparts

---

*In this respect, aspects of the contemporary sociocultural personality of Nigerian individuals and groups can also be traced to the ethnic and religious (Islamic) hierarchical structures of the people's traditions.

in the remote rural areas. Based upon our observations, we hold that the social stratification of some Nigerian mother-tongues, like Yoruba for example, are linked to the hierarchical and authoritarian social structure of traditional culture. Given the traditional social situation, some cultural groups (again Yoruba, for example) were ripe for the hierarchical and authoritarian rule imposed by the British. The devastation of British rule reinforced and gave a new license to the social hegemony of the Nigerian social structure as well as modernized its class formations. But while we concede that social stratification has long existed in traditional relationships and is indeed reflected in the present-day language interchange of mother-tongue users, those who are likely to be considered ideal examples of fluent mother-tongue speakers, but are not competent in English, yield no linguistic capital power (social leverage, etc.) under the present mode of production of Nigeria. Our concern with regard to social stratification in Nigerian language usage is not for symbolic value or the "virtues" of tradtional culture (*gerontocracy, etc.*), but rather for the value which is directly linked to capital power.

Nevertheless, the sociolinguistic setting of present-day urban Nigeria, to which the following "dialogue" belongs, provides communication situations, which reflect through the various levels of language, the antagonism and dialogic of the dehumanizing antidialogue which arises from the interaction of dialectically interrelated sociolinguistic classes.

Our analysis of the "dialogue" is from the perspective of a nonexpert in the field of linguistics. The linguist would probably view our description of the "dialogue" as rather sketchy and wanting - or nearer to a layman's point of view. The linguist would probably employ metrics illustrating the prosodic and graphemic features of language per the syntactical arrangement of the speech, and explain in his jargon the interconnection between these factors and the lexical items and their semantic relevance among the units of the spoken utterance. Such a detailed understanding of language cannot be demonstrated in the following nonexpert analysis.

Our sample of "dialogue" is admittedly an extreme case; certainly more subtle examples exist and perhaps would serve as a greater challenge for our purposes. Nevertheless, this scene, entitled "Day of the Worker," involves a driver, his Oga*, Eskor (a corporate executive) and a Member of Parliament (M.P.). At this point in the play, the three characters come to the shop floor of a factory en route to the Oga's office. The driver angers his Oga by dropping a stack of files which he had been entrusted to carry to the office. In his irritated mood, the Oga seizes the opportunity to scold the driver about his "poor" driving and particularly about his handling of the brakes. These details leading up to the following "dialogue" must be kept in mind in order to understand the full communication situation.

1. Eskor: (To MP) And only moments ago the bum descended so hard on the brakes that I am positive the poor blocks are all worn out.

2. M.P.: I fear for the brake discs.

3. Eskor: Does he, driver that he claims to be, does he even know what brake discs are?. . .

4. Driver: Yes sah.

5. Eskor: What do you mean "yes sah?". . .How much does one cost?. . .I mean only one brake disc of a Mercedes car. . .forget about these other ones which we drive. . .I mean the commonest, the cheapest brand of. . .Mercedes car(s)?. . .

6. M.P.: A 200

7. Eskor: Yes, . . . with which my son in Britain has had to make do for the past three years.

8. Driver: Sorry sah. I don't know sah.

9. Eskor: Did I say you ever knew anything?

10. Driver: Am sorry sah. . .about that files falling on the ground now. . .excuse sah, please sah, let me speak pidgin sah. . .when I just come in before Oga and Oga carring dhis files and Oga brief-case, I see everybody jus dey waka about not knowing Oga is coming with

---

*Yoruba for master.

Oga and I say "Oga dey come for behind" but e dey like say dhat no mean anything for anybody. So I stop for proof say Oga dey come with Oga so make everybody take note. Na so dhe files take fall for ground scatter. Sorry sah.

1. In the first line of the "dialogue" Eskor uses the social selector *bum* in referring to the Driver. The word *bum* is demeaning to the Driver. The term refers to a poor worker or a wandering beggar. Nevertheless, we are not out to prove these ascriptions befitting or nonbefitting of the Driver. Eskor's elaborate use of the English language when describing the Driver's handling of the brakes is, however, worth noting. The structure of the utterance is complex and shows an organization of thought in terms of "time," "degree," and "result" of the action. The verbs may give us some clues about Eskor's pompousness. The verbs in this line of speech are educated and absolute. In the first case we have *descended* as opposed to "braked" or to "slammed" – the more common sayings; in the second we have ⏐ 'am positive ⏐ and third ⏐ are ... worn out ⏐. On another level, beyond its superficial meaning and appearance, this line also reveals the lack of scientific and objective thinking on the part of Eskor; there is no evidence supporting his affirmative assertion that, "the poor blocks are all worn out." This can only be an assumption. Thus the contrast between the lexical word *bum* and the nominal *poor blocks* demonstrates that Eskor places greater value on material things than on human beings. He is insensitive to the Driver and sympathetic to the *poor blocks*.

2. In line two, M.P. is more specific than Eskor; he calls a thing by its name, brake disc. M.P. also shows a greater concern for the car than for the integrity of the Driver.

3.–4. The third and fourth lines are directly related, the first being an interrogative expression prompting the response in the latter. In line three, Eskor insults the occupational integrity and the intelligence of the Driver. The structure of Eskor's question suggests his contempt (mood) for the Driver. There is first a false start, ⏐ ⏐ Does he ⏐ ⏐ and then a nominalization, which is an interpolation, ⏐ ⏐ driver that he claims to be ⏐ ⏐ The nominalization suggests in the verbal group, ⏐ claims to be ⏐ (implying doubt) that Eskor is not convinced that the driver (as theme of the clause) has any right to his title. In addition, Eskor insults the intelligence of the Driver by completing his abuse with the interrogative statement | | does he even know what brake discs are?. . . | | suggesting that knowing what brake discs are is a minimum requisite for any driver, while at the same time implying the Driver's ignorance. In line four the most obvious feature is phonological, that is, the use of /sah/ as opposed to /sir/. This may indicate that a "nonstandard" variety of a Nigerian pronunciation is being used. The Driver's reply (*yes sah*) also tells us that it is quite likely that he knows what brake discs are, but before he is allowed to speak further, his Oga immediately reacts in line five.

5. In line five Eskor's speech becomes more emotive. He first responds to the Driver with two brief (wh) interrogative sentences, | | | What do you mean 'Yes say'? | | | . . . | | | How much does one cost? | | | At this point, Eskor is determined to "dress down" the Driver. Intonation and other prosodic features play an important part in expressing the mood of the speaker. It is our guess that these two interrogative statements are articulated with great stress, indicative of Eskor's surprise at the Driver's reply and of his anger. By now it is clear that Eskor does not intend to exchange words with the Driver. What already appears to be a dehumanizing interchange is continued further down the path of antidialogue.

The following (three) clauses border on being declarative and interrogative, that is, they are statements clarifying the question, ("How much does one cost?") while at the same time they complete the overall interrogative expression. It should be noted that the writer ends this line of "dialogue" with an interrogative punctuation mark. In line five, we also find the repetition of the word *Mercedes*, which serves as a socioeconomic marker and tells us about Eskor's status. When describing the kind of Mercedes he has in mind, (in the last two clauses) Eskor uses the modifiers *commonest* and *cheapest*. From a sociopolitical and a socioeconomic viewpoint we should ask, "*commonest* and *cheapest*" to whom? There is no brand of Mercedes that is common or cheap to those who constitute groups dialectically related to the like of Eskor. In the previous clauses (two and three), we may also infer that in Eskor's opinion, a Mercedes car is below his social standards: | | I mean only one brake disc of a Mercedes car | | . . .

| | *forget about these other ones which we drive. . .* | | (emphasis mine). From the small piece of dialogue before us we can only guess that Eskor is using a Rolls-Royce or a Maserrati, or an even more expensive limousine (whatever it may be).

6. Line six (*A 200*), spoken by M.P., offers little to the dialogue. This line serves as a cue to line seven in which Eskor continues to express condescension.

7. In line seven we discover more about Eskor's socioeconomic status. First of all, we learn that he has a son in Britain – in the Nigerian environment, only those of privilege can afford to travel abroad. The fixed collocation | make do | referring to Eskor's son having to use a Mercedes A 200 implies that the car is too inferior for the son. Most important, Eskor's extravagant taste is far beyond the grasp of the Driver.

8. Line eight, | | | Sorry sah | | | | | | I don't know sah | | | , spoken by the Driver is misleading on the surface. This statement does not necessarily tell us of the Driver's ignorance about brake discs, but instead indicates his powerlessness and his submission to the will of his Oga. The Driver knows that he must play the imbecile that his boss thinks he is if he wants to avoid further humiliation.

If knowing what brake discs are requires more than just knowing what the mechanism does, its location (on the car) and its cost—if it requires actual personal ownership of a Mercedes (or its equivalent), then certainly the Driver could not adequately answer Eskor's question. Looking back to line 3, the verb *know* is loaded with meaning; "does he even *know* what brake discs are?" can be extended to, *has he ever owned one.*

9. In line nine Eskor's reply to the Driver, | | | Did I say you ever knew anything | | | is a stressful, "coldhearted," interrogative statement which reaffirms Eskor's condescension and contempt toward the Driver.

10. The final piece of "dialogue" (line ten) spoken by the Driver is an attempt on the part of the Driver to restore his integrity. The third, fourth and fifth units, "excuse sah," "please sah" "let me speak pidgin sah. . ." reveal that language is of importance to the Driver. He has

been made aware of the difference between his own use of language (pidgin) and his Oga's educated upper-class English. He tries to explain in pidgin his actions and the falling of the files which he had been entrusted to carry. Having already submitted once to his Oga, the Drive attempts to recount the event which annoyed Eskor (the Oga) in the first place, since it was this incident which led to the ensuing abuse. Let us examine the Driver's speech under the headings of vocabulary, structure, and phonology.

Among the Driver's vocabulary, we find the lexical item *Oga*, a Yoruba word for master which is a geolinguistic marker. Thus the being-verb *dey* (an operator), and the preposition *for* (meaning towards), which introduces adverbial phrases indicating place or direction, seem to be common features of the Driver's pidgin.

Now given our standard English background and our knowledge of African American NS English, what can we say is noticeable about the structure of the Driver's pidgin? Let us take, for example this piece of pidgin:

    a. | | I see everybody jus' dey waka about not

    b. knowing Oga is coming with Oga | | and | | I say "Oga dey come for behind" | |

    c. | | but e dey like say dhat no mean anything for anybody | |

We might note in line a. | dey waka | which is similar to the African American | be walkin | and still equivalent to the standard English *walking*. Let us look at the contrast between the verbal phrases below.

Pidgin	*African American NS*
I see everybody 'jus'	I see everybody, dey (they)
dey waka about	'jus' be walkin about

SE
I see (saw) everybody
just walking about

One may key in on the verbalism (line b) ⌐ is coming ¬ marking the Driver's acquisition of an element of standard construction; "dey come," is perceived as a more natural form in pidgin. An additional element of standard English is noticeable in line c in the phrase *no mean anything*. The Driver's usage here is in near proximity to standard English. There is again the almost correct use of the negative *no* (correct = doesn't) and the non-assertive pronoun *anything* as opposed to the general "nonstandard" double-negative (dN) used by African Americans, e.g., *no . . . nothing** Going back to line b, to the specific clause ⌐ ¬ Oga dey come for behind ⌐ ¬ ,we find the formation: subject, verb phrase, adjunct, i.e., Oga ⌐ dey come for behind. Here we can substitute two variants of the verb phrase dey come:

African American NS	*SE*
"be comin"	"is coming"

The adjunct or adverbial phrase ⌐ for behind ⌐ (for = towards) in standard English or in African American NS English would be converted to the following:

SE	*African American NS*
unnatural:	"
The boss is coming behind	The "man's" comin behind
natural:	"
The boss is coming	The "man's" comin . . .

---

*If we take that portion of line c which says *no mean anything for anybody* and translate it to African American NS English, we will have *don't mean nothing to nobody*. Here the negatives are not distinguished from the non-assertive forms. This linguistic phenomenon of total negation runs parallel to the severe social, political and economic alienation of its speakers. It should be noted that the phenomenon of total negation in African American NS English is an acceptable construction in Spanish, e.g., *no significa nada a nadie* (translation) no/signifies (mean)/*nothing/to/nobody*. This accepted form in Spanish raises serious questions for lower-class Hispanic citizens and migrant workers in America who have little or no exposure to English language capital, and who try to acquire standard English.

In addition to other changes, the preposition *for* has been omitted in both cases.

It should be noted that the preposition *for* is in line c proceeding the indefinite pronoun (complement) *anybody*, which in this instance is a correct usage* of the non-assertive form although *to* would be the more appropriate preposition.

Probably the most impressive use of adverbials in the Driver's speech is contained in the sentence| | | Na so the files take fall for ground scatter| | | in which the adverbialization not only tells us where the files fell, but also how they dispersed on contact with the ground.

In addition to the Driver's use of /sah/ as opposed to /sir/, he frequently substitutes *d* for the (continuant) phoneme *th*:

Pidgin (and African Amer. NS)	SE
dhis also *dis*	*this*
dhat also *dat*	*that*
dhe i.e., *dhi* or *de*	*the*

In the opening utterances of this portion of the "dialogue" (line 10), the Driver uses the standard *that*, which indicates that the correct pronunciation is known to him. As far as phonological deviations are concerned vis-à-vis the continuant /th/, it sometimes seems as if a conscious deanglicization is taking place. We see the same in the use of *the* in the same line. This might also represent an inconsistency on the part of the playwright.

Throughout the Driver's speech we see a demonstration of *verbal control*. We can infer from the overall communication situation that the tone of the Driver's discourse imbibes the respect and courtesy afforded to an ascending class figure in an antagonistic and yet powerless confrontation of a lower-class laborer with his bourgeois counterpart.

In this analysis, we have attempted to show the uncompromising domination of the privileged bourgeoisie (notwithstanding some

---

*Such as in: "There are no Cadillacs for anybody."

individual exceptions in real life), over the lower-class through the medium of language. Condescension and/or contempt on the part of the upper-class speaker when engaged in a communication situation with members of the lower class appear to be the major features of the discourse. We have also shown expressed powerlessness with regard to the Driver (as a representative of the lower class). What we could not demonstrate in our analysis is expressed defiance of the lower class (reverse antagonism), which is as well manifested in the production relationship between *Haves* and *Have-nots*. In addition, one can also describe, in more subtle examples, the paternalistic character of bourgeois discourse in the verbal interchange of dialectically interconnected class groups.

Although few words were exchanged between Eskor and M.P. (the Member of Parliament), we can infer that given the fact that they share the same class strata, there would be a high level of compromise and mutual respect between the two.

The sociolinguistic manifestations of class dialectics do not explain all there is to say about social antagonism through the medium of language; certainly racial, sexual, and ethnic stigmas also play their parts. Of these three elements, let us look at the question of race.

Where racial formations are of great significance and determine relationships between groups, language may stigmatize a race (the underdog) even in situations where on the most obvious level there is mutuality of class. Take for example an encounter between a Euro-American policeman (a judicial agent of the bourgeoisie) and an African American physician and professor of psychology, the nationally famous Dr. Alvin Poussaint of Harvard University (a member of the intelligentsia). One can assume that each participant earns a salary exceeding $20,000 per annum and certainly in this instance the African American earns more than the Euro-American. Susan Ervin-Tripp provides the following "dialogue" and the ensuing analysis of this antagonistic linguistic interchange between races:

'What's your name, boy?'
'Dr. Poussaint. I'm a physician.'
'What's your first name, boy?'
'Alvin.'
The policeman insulted Dr. Poussaint three times. First, he

employed a social selector for race in addressing him as 'boy,' which neutralizes identity set, rank and even adult status. If addressed to a white, 'boy' presumably would be used only for a child, youth or menial regarded as a nonperson. (See Fishman, p. 22)

Before moving to the second insult, what Ervin-Tripp says in this last sentence, which refers to the implied meaning of 'boy' if addressed to a white, needs some clarification. The first explanation is scientific, chronological. The second, however, is social, economic, and political, and is counterprogressive because it is a stigma on labor or, to put it another way, it is a stigma on legitimate forms of participation in the collective productivity of human beings. Ervin-Tripp goes on to say that:

The officer next treated TLN (title and last name), as failure to answer his demand, as a non-name, and demanded FN (first name); third, he repeated the term 'boy' which would be appropriate to unknown addressees. (Ibid)

(Notwithstanding the fact that the addressee had given his last name and title.)

In the opinion of the policeman, "Blacks are wrong to claim adult status or occupational rank. (They) are children." (Ibid) It should be noted that African Americans are the largest group of peoples of color and constitute a vast portion of the lower class in the United States.

The social selector 'boy' can be further explained as a class stigma. For instance, in Nigeria a messenger, vulcanizer, steward, or driver of legal adult age is often called *boy* when referred to or addressed (usually for service) by some, and indeed many, upper-class members of the society. *Boy* here is synonymous to *a menial regarded as a nonperson.*

Pidgins, "Nonstandards" and the Politics of Cross-Cultural and Cross-Class Scholarship

At this junction we will speak to a kind of false consciousness associated with the notions of elaborated codes of sophistication and control-standards, and restricted codes of so-called "cultural deficit"—"nonstandards" or pidgins. The former are considered superior and the latter inferior. The stigma articulated to so-called restricted codes, and the importance and decisive function given to elaborated codes fall into the dialectical realm of over determinism. Where in social relations linguistic competence is articulated to the mode of production (to its material base), speech and literacy, acquired through formal training in the dominant institution, are two of many determinants (determinisms) affecting the organization of material life. Here we shall attempt, specifically, to undercut the notions of "elaborated" and "restricted" codes, and demystify meta language.

Pidgin* is an old commercial language originally associated with the Anglo-Chinese and later associated with other European colonies in Africa and other parts of the world where Western imperialists conducted trade with others whose languages did not

---

*In Western and Northern Nigeria, where Yoruba and Hausa, respectively, linguistically unite the population, the pidgin-speaking sector is comparatively limited. In the western area we expect to find pidgin in brewery towns like Ilesa, in university towns like Ife and Ilorin, and in big cities like Lagos and Ibadan. Similarly, in the north we can find pidgin in university towns (where there are foreigners and a mixture of indigenous citizens) like Jos and Zaria, and in big cities like Kano and Kaduna. However, pidgin is more widely spoken in mid-western and eastern Nigeria where the multilingual population demands it as a linqua franca. Notwithstanding, pidgin is not simply used because a community is linguistically diversified, but also because for many people it is the first stage in acquiring English.

allow for mutually intelligible communication between the imperialists and their clients. Since the beginning of European imperialism in Africa, Asia and Latin America, pidgins have become more than just commercial languages of imperialism; today imperialists no longer rely on these media, as they used to. Pidgins are now linqua francas serving to bridge the linguistic gap between peoples belonging to a common federation or republic, but at the same time are of different language groups.

Some pidgin studies have gone as far as to say that pidgins are not necessarily or exclusively linked to the standard lexis of European languages but are also linked to non-European standards (see Hymes 1968). Indeed, studies of pidgins have caused much controversy. Pidgins comprise simple and common words of a superposed language, lexical items of indigenous tongues, plus traces of an authentic lexis and flexibly adapted mother-tongue grammatical structures and occasional standard constructs, which reflect the cognitive codes of the speakers.

If we look at "pidgin English," that is, pidgin of Anglophone colonies (see patois)* as a deanglicized English, it might be permissible to call it a restricted code of that language (English), if one can convincingly say that the pidgin of such areas are actually forms of English. Anglophone pidgin is indeed unintelligible to native speakers of English and seems to stand as a separate language. Pidgins do not rely on the standard constructs of superposed, nonindigenous languages and although they may engage in lexical borrowing from these languages, pidgins are no more dialects or substandards of superposed, nonindigenous languages than English is of Latin or Greek.

What pidgins have in common with the so-called restricted and "sub/nonstandard" varieties of standard languages is that both are associated with illiteracy and the lower class. Thus both are related to

---

*In English patois is no different from dialect. However, to the French, dialects are local languages without orthography and if allowed to linger in that state become patois. This implies that the pidgin of Nigeria is a patois, that is, since we have not agreed on any transcription of it.

colonialism, except the first is directly associated with imperialism, while the second is a domestic-intranational form. And in addition to this, both are under attack by cross-cultural scholarship.

The terminology "nonstandard" seems to be associated with the absence of prescribed script communication—which is nowadays the most crucial determinant of "standard" (educated) language. The problem with the terms "nonstandard" and "standard" is that so many linguistic communities which have no written form of language also have high status and low status varieties which are, in some instances, referred to as "standards" and "nonstandards" respectively. In pre-World War II Nigeria, and specifically in the Yoruba speaking territories, speakers located in cultural and commercial centers like Oyo and Ife, on the one hand, and Ijebu and Ibadan on the other, would be users of high status Yoruba, while other Yoruba groups in the remote areas would be users of a low status variety. It would appear in this instance that the labels "standard" and "nonstandard" are more relevant to the degree of cultural capital in a language variety than to the importance of prescribed script communication; Yoruba script is a post-World War II phenomenon. The contemporary use of terms like "standard" and "nonstandard" marks a misconception and bias of present-day European cross-cultural and cross-class scholarship. Such terms give little concession to the eloquent speech of an Ifa priest who hails from Oyo or to the continuum of dialects and creole-pidgins.

It is a reasonable proposition that African American "nonstandard" English has a history dating back to slavery and that the mother tongues of African slaves at some early stage converged with the English of plantation owners and overseers. Nowadays, however, it is argued that there are no significant remnants of African mother-tongues in African American speech with the exception of perhaps the French Creole in Louisiana or Gullah (or Geeche) spoken along the coastline of South Carolina, Georgia and northeast Florida. These however are dying creoles. Present arguments hold that African American "nonstandard" speech is a low status variety in the monolingual diaglossia of American speech. It is no more than a dialect of poverty, and this type of speech is also present among poor whites, although there are understandably, colloquial differences. Notwithstanding, in a diachronic study from the streets of old

England through slavery to the present, the speech commonly and generally referred to as Black English (African American "nonstandard" English) is likely to be an excellent example of dialect continuum.

From another vantage point all together, it could be said that pidgins are imperial and colonial "bastardizations" of indigenous tongues, contrary to the reverse. One can even go further to say that there is mutual "bastardization" of all the component languages which compromise pidgin. But above all the validity of the terminology "bastardization" needs to be questioned whenever the term is applied to languages with traditions and we hold that all languages have traditions.

Moving now to a different plane, we often ponder whether pidgins or any so-called "nonstandard" variety is actually restricted, though we know in linguistic terms what this means. Restricted in what sense? Is this a useless debate of langue and parole? Because the status quo languages of sophistication are full with subordinate clauses, adjectives, adverbs, tenses, etc., are we to hold that all languages must engage these agents in the same way as status quo varieties do? We should recognize, however, that the syntactical and lexical elaboration of languages, along with the synchronous development of science, numerals and the alphabet (around the Mediterranean areas of Asia and Africa), and their importance vis-à-vis the conquering nationalities of Europe gets down to the historical and ethnological essence of Western standard varieties' capital value and "superiority." Thus the state and private distribution of language capital (status quo varieties) in a class system control the expected "demand-pull" inflation of the linguistic supply in such a way that social classes share unequal value resulting in conditions of privilege on the one hand and poverty on the other. The first is a state of inclusion, and the second a state of exclusion in relation to the socio-politico-economic mainstream. The worst of this is the general demoralizing conscience behind the dichotomy.

In addressing the previous question, "Restricted in what sense?", let us turn again to an earlier cited passage from Jerome Bruner, which implied that only standard languages have the capacity to accommodate analytic and synthetic reasoning, which seems to imply that the broad community of "nonstandard" language users do not codify their perceptions and interpretations of events or complex problems,* as if, for example, metaphoric constructions, generally associated with African American English, do not demonstrate a level of abstract symbolization, mediated by the world reality (or "cultural code") of the speaker. It is observed that: "Ethnotropic** utterances (widely used in Black culture) generate the capacity to liberate rather than confine creative powers in discourse." (Holt, p. 9)

> This capacity is . . . the generative power relationship between metaphor and symbol which gives the metaphor the power to fill its own cup of meaning and spill over. [It is] the dialectical process whereby metaphor conjoins 'Thesis' and 'anti-thesis' to bring [about] 'synthesis' [and this] is the very process whereby discourse comes into being. (W. Ross Winterowd cited by Holt, Ibid.)

There is seemingly an aim toward "decontextualization" in the metaphor in African American speech which tends to make it ambiguous.*** However, "The essential ambiguity of metaphor [in African American speech] is usually resolved [as Bruner has indicated] by the contextual clues, convergent concepts, knowledge and expectations of members of the culture. In conventional standard usage one is taught to avoid ambiguous metaphors for they obscure literal meaning." (Ibid, p. 3)

---

*This is a cross-culture notion which has also been imposed on African languages and traditional thought. Although this notion is constantly under attack, and put on the defense, many Africanist scholars, who engage in cross-cultural arguments, then go to the extreme of either being romantically noncritical of African tradition, or those who are critical too often project reactionary-preservative tendencies when addressing the "African tradition" question. In addition to this, some Africanist scholars have claimed that African thought, being context and consensus bound, and being unrecorded lacks innovation (see brief comment by Mazrui in *World Culture and the Black Experience* (p. 65). Understandably this notion is transferred to some Western percepts of African languages.

**Ethnotropism is the use of a word or expression in a different cultural sense from that which belongs to it for the purposes of *giving life* or *emphasis* to an idea. (see Holt, p. 14)

***There are implied and inferred meanings as well as suppositions in bourgeois literature.

Within the domain of "nonstandard" varieties, the capacity of users to decontextualize these languages is an on-going process of their development. Lower or working-class communities do not exist in absolute ignorance of, or in complete isolation from, the world around them and are in daily contact with other sociolinguistic communities and classes. Like any other speech community, lower-class, "nonstandard" speech communities are capable of generating new words and concepts, or borrowing them from elsewhere when the verbal-symbolization of experiences outside the collective or individual context is needed. Although it would be politically naive to compare the lexes of "nonstandard" languages to standards and expect to find "equality," not enough is known about the range of "nonstandard" lexes or their rate of growth, (this is primarily true with pidgins) since these languages are generally spoken and seldom written and have no dictionaries of standard spelling, pronunciation or use. In addition to this problem, there is the fact that no two individual speakers have the same vocabulary range.

In spite of the "observations" of Western (or bourgeois) cross-cultural and cross-class scholarship, which has confused the relationship between decontextualization and consensus*, consensus orientation, often associated with lower-class speech, seems to be the kernel of *the word* and of defining the world. Social consensus and the consensus orientation of language have their own dialectic of reaction and action, or shall we say, "of oppression and liberation." If as a result of ideological and material contradictions and changes, consensus guided by "true dialogue" is shaped so as to generate acts of liberation in individuals of oppressed communities, a new character of language and a whole new movement of liberating innovations might persist. Let us consider the rather Althusserian (See Larraine, pp. 154-164) chart below illustrating the position of consensus and language, from a sociopolitical point of view, keeping in mind the role of "human

---

*Decontextualization is a movement towards providing a sophisticated worldwide view in the framework of local consensus. Language has two faces: one reflects the notion of the self and the other reflects the local context in relations to the world around it. At the most basic level, this explains how all communities establish consensus (reactionary or progressive) about outsiders.

consciousness and *the Word*," "class objectives," and "innovations" and the dialectical nature of class consciousness and class struggle.

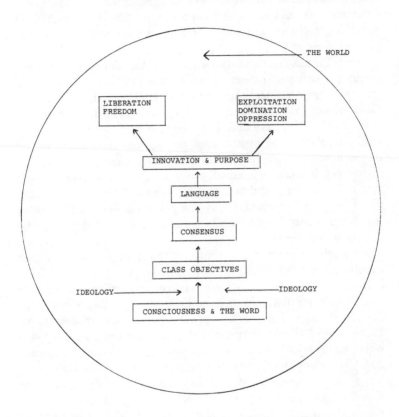

Social history shows evidence of shared consensus between progressive bourgeois elements (dialogical and dialectical men and women) and the oppressed, and the rhetorical style of the African American leader Malcolm X demonstrates this language. Malcolm X was one of the few African American intellectuals who, through his many public speeches, communicated effectively (not shy of similes, metaphors, slang or narration) his revolutionary ideas in a near-grassroot language, to grassroot people. Malcolm employed the consensus-oriented devices of Black discourse in an attempt to achieve a revolutionary consensus within and among different oppressed African communities throughout the United States. Where decontextualization and consensus come together here, is in Malcolm's internationalist and nationalist approach to addressing the African American problem and the problems of the world's oppressed peoples. This was his style of pedagogy.

One of the most memorable things about Malcolm's speeches is the frequent opening statement, "Let's git down to business today in a language everybody here can understand" (or something thereabout). Here Malcolm communicates a strategy as well as a statement.

Further to all we have said about "nonstandard" varieties, we have observed an analytical, synthetic and philosophical meta-talk produced by pidgin speakers as representative of a lower-class, "nonstandard" vernacular. It would be interesting to observe how a speaker of pidgin would discuss the postulates, "I think, therefore I am," and "I feel, therefore I am," or observe how one pidgin speaker would explain the process of smelting metals to his counterpart (the receiver) who has no knowledge of the subject.

Although we have no experiment of the second proposition, our experiment in relations to the two postulates, (1) *I think, therefore I am* and (2) *I feel, therefore I am*, has rendered striking results. The first postulate is taken from Rene Descartes and the second from Leopold Senghor. The backdrop of our experiment is explained in Ali Mazrui's book *World Culture and the Black Experience* (pp. 48-49) where he deals with the contest between the world views of Europe and Africa using Descartes and Senghor as representatives of the two universes respectively. Mazrui also brings into this discussion Kwame Nkrumah as he refers to Nkrumah's book *Consciencism* where Descartes' postulate is also discussed. Mazrui summarizes Nkrumah's assessment of Descartes, "I think, therefore I am." Says Mazrui:

> Nkrumah argues that the fact that 'Monsieur Descartes is thinking is no proof that his body exists. It is certainly no proof that the totality of his person is in being.' Nkrumah is out to deny that matter owes its existence either to thought or to perception. In a sense he would disagree with both reasonings, 'I think, therefore I am' and 'I feel, therefore I am.' But to the extent that 'feeling' is a more physical

experience than thought, it is a greater concession to the autonomy of matter. The kind of philosophical idealism that puts our bodies in our minds instead of our minds in our bodies was to Nkrumah no more that an indulgence in 'the ecstacy of intellectualism.' (pp. 48-49)

As we are not interested in proving the superiority of either Descartes' position or Senghor's, Mazrui's reference to Nkrumah's assessment of Descartes is not intended to give a narrow-minded stamp of approval to Senghor. After the above quotation Mazrui goes on to say that:

... Nkrumah would certainly not go to the extent of denying the African the gift of analytical and discursive reason. As he himself put it at the inauguration of the University of Ghana in November 1961, 'We have never had any doubt about the intellectual capacity of the African.' (p. 49)

To Nkrumah, both Descartes and Senghor have missed the total point.

The concern of our experiment is for the analytical, synthetic, and philosophical capacity of pidgin language spoken by peasants and working class people. The entire recorded experiment is 27 minutes long, and the portion we have extracted for the purposes of this discussion is 3 minutes long and our present transcription covers about half of the latter.

The participants in the experiment are (first speaker) Mr. Augustine Nwaiwu* and (second speaker) Mr. Stephenson Nwosu**. Neither of the two have higher education training but have some exposure to upper-class English and are functionally literate. We were assisted in

---

*Mr. Nwaiwu is from eastern Nigeria. He is a former steward then employed in Oduduwa Hall at the University of Ife. Mr. Nwaiwu is one of many young Nigerians struggling for admission to the university.

**Mr. Nwosu is also from eastern Nigeria, and has a wife and six children. He is an occasional steward and former taxi driver, who was briefly employed as a driver at the University of Ife. During the period in which this experiment took place, Mr. Nwosu was employed in an agricultural project in Ilesa.

this experiment by Mr. Rufus Orishayomi*, who performed most of the transcribing but was not present at the actual taping. The portion of the experiment which follows only includes the first speaker, Mr. Nwaiwu. Although there was substantial agreement between Mr. Nwaiwu and Mr. Nwosu, we believe that there is every possibility that the first speaker influenced the second. We had assumed that this discussion would take the form of a debate. We might add here that our own participation in the experiment as a participant-learner-observer was extremely limited so as not to influence the main participants. We introduced each of the postulates without revealing their original sources and without providing any background information about them. After it was agreed that the discussion was finished, we then explained to Mr. Nwaiwu and to Mr. Nwosu the background details of the experiment. No portion of this explanation (or the participants' reaction to it, although quite interesting) has been used in the present extract. The most crucial rule governing the exercise was that the speaker must try as best he could to speak throughout in pidgin without switching to elements of status quo English.

Although we will not translate Mr. Nwaiwu's pidgin analysis to status quo "Nigerian English," we will lay out his discussion in such a way that it is easily understood.

The basic conclusion vis-à-vis postulate (1), I think, therefore I am, is summed up in the following way by Mr. Nwaiwu:

a. He think dey for mind
b. himself dey confused
c. someone don convince im
d. say he bi so

Let us look at Mr. Nwaiwu's analysis:

e. himself come say for in mind
f. he think say dhe person
g. he say befor he say dis one

---

*Mr. Orishayomi holds a post-graduate diploma in film and television from Middlesex Poly-Technique, London. He has authored two plays in pidgin, "Poor Dey Suffer" and "E No Go Happen To Me" (unpublished), both of which were performed at the African Center in Covent Garden (London) in 1980.

(pointing to the last clause, "I am," on a sheet of paper)
i. something for don happen wey make im
j. say therefore to dhat person wey
k. e talk wit im
l. wey he come convince him
m. he say-im him surrender
n. he say okay I hope I bi so . . .

We can assess Mr. Nwaiwu's analysis of postulate one from the following angles: First, he is not convinced that thinking is enough to explain existence; according to Mr. Nwaiwu, Descartes "hopes" he exists (i.e., line n, "I hope I bi so"). Second, Mr. Nwaiwu is also concerned with the structure of the postulate, and particularly with the conjunctive adverb *therefore*. To Mr. Nwaiwu *therefore* indicates that something has taken place and has influenced Descartes' conclusion that he exists. To him the action which has previously occurred is more than the mental act of thinking. Mr. Nwaiwu brings into the picture a second party who has actually convinced Descartes of his existence. What this means is that in Mr. Nwaiwu's opinion, some physical or speech activity must have occurred; in other words, thinking is a reaction to verbal interchange or to physical experience.

The basic conclusion vis-à-vis postulate (2), *I feel, therefore I am*, is summed up by Mr. Nwaiwu as follows:
o. him look around

(he gestures, stroking the right arm with the left hand and the left arm with the right hand)*
p. him bi say

The analysis for postulate (2) proceeds in the following way:
q. himself too, he feel he say
r. e for don get some "effidence" for himself

---

*We regret that this experiment was conducted in such a way that the speaker was not isolated alone in a room. It is believed that the speaker would have been more verbally explicit if others were not present. It should be noted, however, that throughout his discussion, Mr. Nwaiwu gestures only thrice.

s. wi make im feel say e bi so
t. dhat person too, "therefore" be dhere
u. dhat person too don win im small
v. he surrender himself small
w. but he no fit surrender
x. he give him some "effidence"
y. dhat he must believe. . .

As for postulate (2) Mr. Nwaiwu holds that feeling implies physical proof of existence, and in this way he agrees with Nkrumah's assessment of Descartes' postulate. When dealing with postulate (2) Mr. Nwaiwu is also concerned with the conjunctive adverb *therefore*, and when discussing this postulate deals with the second party which he mentioned earlier. He holds that the man who *feels* need not be persuaded by others that he exists; his existence is determined by sensory perception.

It is important to recognize that Mr. Nwaiwu's overall analysis, and particularly his concern for the conjunctive adverb *therefore*, and the bringing into focus the second party, in a sense, goes beyond Mazrui's reference to Nkrumah's assessment. Mr. Nwaiwu's allusion to the second party illustrates the philosophy that the question of existence is only significant in relationship to others. Consequently the question of being is a human question and the verification of one's being can only be had as a result of the interaction of human consciousness. Inasmuch as the question of existence (being) is a human one, Mr. Nwaiwu establishes an implied agreement with Mazrui's interpretation of Nkrumah, i.e., denying "that matter owes its existence either to thought or to perception." (page 48) In the final analysis, Mr. Nwaiwu's comments are an emphatic rejection of *solipsism*.

Jerome Bruner, J. B. Pride, and Basil Bernstein would probably argue that the treatment of these postulates would be overly simplified and that the verbal performance would not demonstrate "linguistic self-sufficiency." Pride would argue that the "nonstandard," lower-class speaker (or those suffering from code restriction), would be reliant on paralinguistic and extraverbal features, suggesting that such features are indicative of lower quality communication. This, however, is not major to our observation. But to this we say that we recognize linguistic self-sufficiency without making "linguistic stepchildren" of paralinguistic and extraverbal features.

In fact, studies have shown that if one were to pay normal attention to a recorded sample of unrehearsed every-day-casual speech, one would hear several false starts, pauses, idiolectal phrases, and evidence of mental backtracking regardless of the class status of the speakers. If one does not hear the tape several times and if one does not attempt to imagine the situation and actions of the speakers, the recorded sample is hardly comprehensible. What is operating here is the importance of situation and the use of paralinguistic features. These external features of communication are not exclusive to the "speech" of the lower class; even the meta-languages of status quo "scripts" rely on metrics in order to achieve greater understanding.*

In summing up this discussion let us say that if one overreacts to the syndrome of elaborated code superiority, as, for example, Bernstein, Bruner and Pride do, in the long run will see nothing worthwhile or "universal" (to us an untimely word), about "nonstandard" varieties or about the humanity of "nonstandard" speakers.

---

*It is true that educated varieties are more independent of paralinguistic and extraverbal features, and can rely upon modals, grammatical constructs, etc., to convey attitude and achieve understanding. It should be noted, however, that the demonstration of "pure" grammatical competence is a situational phenomenon, that is, it is usually exercised on formal occasions such as when lecturing or in situations where two educated speakers are not acquainted with one another. Under casual and friendly circumstances grammatical competence or linguistic self-sufficiency is of little concern to even educated speakers. Since "nonstandard" speakers are alienated from most formal situations, and since "nonstandards" are populace languages, there is little need to be concerned about the ramifications of grammatical competence or linguistic self-sufficiency. This, however, does not imply a deficit in verbal interchange. There must be some established rules governing the structure of any language ("standard" or "nonstandard") before there can be intelligibility.

The Political Economy of Culture Capital: Language, Education and the Appropriation of Surplus Value

Political economy is the study of the production relationships in a given, historically-determined society, in its genesis, its development and its decay. Political economy is the science of the laws governing the production and exchange of the material forces of production and subsistence in human society (Gould, p. 72).

Surplus value (s) is a fundamental economic concept. It is the amount of value (unpaid capital) in addition to the initial Capital (C) advanced for industrial production, etc. Here Capital or production comprise constant capital (c) plus variable capital (v)—the cost of materials and labor respectively. Surplus (s)—a concept that goes beyond an understanding of mere profit—is the equivalent of v percentage (or more). Surplus is the unpaid equivalent of v (or labor cost) that is s/v. If Capital = c₦410 plus v₦90 (= ₦500) and s = ₦90, in actuality v is doubled to equal ₦180, with ₦90 representing "living" or necessary labor power and an additional ₦90 representing "dead" (or surplus) labor or the surplus value of products (s90/v90). Hence the total equation becomes P (Production) = s/c+v. The amount subtracted from the true value of labor and commodities, and the nature of this process under capitalism, is the evidence of "exploitation." In a whole working day a laborer works one half of the day for himself and the other half for his employer. (See *Capital*, I, pp. 206-207)*

Surplus value does not evidence exploitation simply because it is capital over and above production cost; in our view, surplus value is a necessary element in the structure of production, and in the development of the political state. Exploitation is connected to surplus value

---

*See also C. Aronson and M. Meo, trans. *A Prospectus for Marx's Mathematical Manuscripts* (Oakland, California: Marx's Mathematical Manuscripts, 1982)

only in terms of social relations and social reproduction resulting from the subsequent appropriation of surplus value itself. (Ibid)

"Marx does not arrive at his results by simple logical abstraction, but by the penetration of the essence of the social relations of capitalism. This penetration requires the dialectical method which alone is capable of respecting the complexities and contradictions in reality." (Cutter, et al, p. 73) In the words of I.I. Rubin*, "The category of 'value' is a part of the law of distribution of social labour and not simply a means of accounting for the exchangeability of all commodities." (Ibid)

Rubin goes on to say that:

Marx analyzes the act of exchange only to the extent that it plays a specific role in the process of reproduction and is closely connected with that process. Marx's theory of value does not analyse every exchange of things, but only that exchange which takes place: (1) *in a commodity society*, (2) among autonomous *commodity producers*, (3) when it is connected with the *process of reproduction* in a determined way, thus representing one of the phases of the process of reproduction. The interconnection of the processes of exchange and distribution of labour in production leads us . . . to concentrate on the value of products of labour (as opposed to natural goods which have a price . . .), and then only on those products which can be reproduced. (Ibid, pp. 73-74)

The motivating purposes of capitalist appropriation of surplus value are improving, expanding and ultimately monopolizing production, devising more effective marketing strategies, appeasing and suppressing social unrest via philanthropic and welfarist institutions and programming the public and replicating the bourgeoisie via education. Certainly the greater portion of surplus capital is refunnelled into production and nowadays in older, more experienced capitalist countries like the United States, the amount of surplus capital expended for philanthropic and welfarist purposes is written off as charitable tax deductions. However, our concern here is with that

---

*See I.I. Rubin, *Essays on Marx's Theory of Value*, pp. 62 and 100-101

amount of capital invested in the perpetuation of superstructure, which includes language and education, inaccessible to the masses.

It is the motive and purpose (monopoly, reproduction and profit) of capitalist appropriation of surplus value that is the concern or central theme of this work. Thus it is on the basis of this concern and central theme that we pose our argument with regard to the question of the "accessibility" of cultural capital in the form of language and education in a class system. As the sociolinguist Basil Bernstein puts it:

> It is not capital, in the strict economic sense, which is subject to appropriation, manipulation and exploitation, but also *cultural capital* in the form of the symbolic systems [i.e., language and education], through which man can extend and change the boundaries of his experiences. (p. 103)

Maybe some examples of the appropriation, manipulation and exploitation of cultural capital as manifestations of surplus capital are needed at this juncture; and some of the best examples are found in American history.

The 1820 census was the first United States document to include the nationalities of Americans. Twenty percent of a population of 9,638,000 were African American, while the remaining eighty percent were of Anglo Saxon stock. Between this time and 1960 over forty million immigrants from Europe and Canada came to the United States. (Rose, p. 37) These new Americans constituted a labor force (particularly along the eastern seaboard) that would soon become a most crucial factor in the American industrial revolution, in the expansion of monopoly capitalism, and in the growing sophistication of social control.

The peak years of European immigration to the United States range from 1851 to 1924. These immigrants included a multitude of about 24 nationalities, most of whom were unskilled laborers and non-English speaking. The Czechs were the smallest group among them, while the Germans constituted the largest of all these nationalities. (Ibid., p. 44)

Interesting enough it is during this period of European immigration—this latter half of the 19th century, the period of reconstruction and of industrial revolution—that private industries in the United States invested (in considerable portion) their surplus capital in custodial institutions established for the purpose of socializing immigrant labor with Anglo-Saxon ethics and indoctrinating them with "democratic capitalist" ideology and values. The devastating aspect of this brainwashing is the acceptance of the basic principle that personal failure is always the fault of the individual, and never the "system."

In the rush to monopolize and dominate the whole industrial and commercial sector, the industrialist bourgeoisie set out to program the "developing" American public into accepting capitalist domination even to the extent of defending it with legislation and the U.S. constitution, and even with their lives.

One of the most popular examples of how industrialists used their surplus capital to further the ideology, philosophy and ultimately the sociology of capitalist domination can be seen in the philanthropic deeds of Andrew Carnegie*, who during the latter half of the 19th century supported the establishment of several libraries along the eastern seaboard, so as to "enlighten" the "ignorant" immigrants. The books that were shelved in these libraries accommodated that purpose.

The African American intelligentsia will long remember Andrew Carnegie's generous support to the "wizard of Tuskegee," Booker T. Washington, who was out to promote vocational skills (likewise passivity) as the Black strategy for the reconstruction period and with the financial help of Carnegie, John D. Rockefeller, H.H. Rogers, Andrew Mellon, Julius Rosenwald, et al, founded Tuskegee Institute and launched several other projects in African American communities.

The finance and appropriation of cultural capital during the industrial revolution, although it may have seemed diabolical to the aware pioneer Marxist in Europe at that time, was perhaps one of the greatest expressions of charity and social concern to the contemporary philanthropist and to the contemporary labor force in the United States. Thus in the light of all this, it is difficult to imagine (through all the American dreams), the toil of child labor in the sweatshops of

---

*Carnegie's voluntary support of vital institutions established to socialize the American classes occurred during a time in American history when there was virtually no tax system let alone opportunity for any charitable tax deduction.

American industries during this period of lax labor legislation. The violence has been removed in present texts.

As there were financiers of cultural capital (some from the internal elite of ethnic groups), during the said period, there were also custodians in charge of its appropriation—manufacturers and retailers of the symbolic products of capital: educationalists and civic leaders whose ideas about America's future were compatible with industry. The educationalists, in collusion with the business sector, pushed for educational reform in the big industrialized cities so as to shape production relationships according to production needs and at the same time promote the cosmetics of capitalist democracy. Martin Carnoy's description of these educational reformists deserves special noting. According to Carnoy:

> By 1900, the reformers were successful in almost every large city. The educators who led this movement often became big city school superintendents. The new boards were controlled by old-stock first citizens, often professionals and businessmen. They did standardize education, but . . . standardized education was geared to differentiate children by the adult occupational roles they were measured to be fit for. [This is not to mention racial and ethnic prejudices.] The professionals and businessmen had an anti-immigrant and antiworking-class attitude which underlay most of their . . . reform. (p. 247).

Nowadays the role played by high level petty bourgeois educationalists and scholars from all areas of academia (Coleman, Conant, Silberman, Moynihan, Katz, Friedman, Kissinger, Brezinzki, etc.) has been the concern of most dialectically aware and critical thinking individuals who have committed themselves to exposing the contradictions of America's class system. The American system of education is indeed the most important instrument of industrial research, of social control and of socialization into the "production - consumption" patterns of the American society. And this is the very reason why the education system is so important to private industry and the state.

> . . . it must suffice to point out that academic qualifications [this includes linguistic competence] are to cultural capital what money is to economic capital. By giving the same value to all holders of the same certificate, so that any one of them can take the place of any

other, the educational system minimizes the obstacles to the free circulation of cultural capital which result from its being incorporated in individual persons (without, however, sacrificing the advantages of the charismatic ideology of the irreplaceable individual); it makes it possible to relate all qualification-holders (and also, negatively, all unqualified individuals) to a single standard, thereby setting up a *single market* for all cultural capacities and guaranteeing the convertibility of cultural capital into money, at a determinant cost in labour and time. Academic qualifications, like money, have a conventional, fixed value which, being guaranteed by law, is freed from local limitations (in contrast to scholastically uncertified cultural capital) and temporal fluctuations: the cultural capital which they in a sense guarantee once and for all does not constantly need to be proved. The objectification accomplished by academic degrees and diplomas and, in a more general way, by all forms of credentials, is inseparable from the objectification which the law guarantees by defining *permanent positions* which are distinct from the biological individuals holding them, and may be occupied by agents who are biologically different but interchangeable in terms of the qualifications required. Once this state of affairs is established, relations of power and domination no longer exist directly between individuals; they are set up in pure objectivity between institutions, i.e., between socially guaranteed qualifications and socially defined positions, and through them, between the social mechanisms which produce and guarantee both the social value of the qualifications and the positions and also the distribution of these social attributes, among biological individuals. (Bourdieu, pp. 187-188)

Anytime the educational system is under attack, and there is a call for radical change or for its abandonment, a portion of industrial surplus capital, which is nowadays funnelled into foundation organizations, is made available to distinguished educationalists and/or scholars who explain away the faults of the system. For example, "Carnegie Foundation sponsored a study by James Conant (1964)*,

---

*See James Conant, *The Education of American Teachers*, New York: McGraw-Hill Book Company, 1963. (Also see Sarason, pp. 26-28)

educationalist and former president of Harvard University, who in effect said the educational system was basically sound but then co-opted the rhetoric of the system's attackers to recommend limited change." (Carnoy, p. 265) Conant suggested better teacher-training as the solution to America's education problem. Again in the 1970s, "when most manpower projections clearly indicated a surplus of labor for the next decade Carnegie Foundation supported a study by Silberman* [who suggested the open classroom] which in effect said that the system was basically sound but needed some reforming." (Ibid.)

Both Conant's and Silbermans's reforms further legitimized a pyramidal class structure and hierarchical relations in production. Where and whenever the efficiency of social control and production are threatened, a portion of surplus capital is used to sponsor experts to suggest the necessary steps to keep the overall system in order.

In the specific case of language, corporate interest has dictated the standard of communication competence and English specialists in the areas of composition and technical writing have been exposed to a multimillion dollar market in which their knowledge is packaged and sold to the executive training programs of big industry (see *Time* magazine, 19 May 1980, pp. 64-65). When we say that language is "cultural capital," we are recognizing its value as a device of opportunity, but moreover, the importance given to language by the corporate elite is even more worthy of noting when we hear a senior vice president of the First Atlantic Corporation asserting that, if he could choose one degree for the people he hired, it would be in English (*Time* magazine, 4 May 1981, p. 38). From the very beginning, the development of language has been determined by economic production and growth.

In America, perhaps it might be said that with compulsory public school education from primary through secondary school, education and as well the elaborate codes of meta-languages are made accessible to everyone. However, we cannot overlook the fact that at various points in American history nonmainstream and non-Anglo sectors of the society have charged that public schools represent an ascending cultural imposition determined by Anglo-Saxon, "founding fathers," superiority and prejudice. The reaction of the lower-class groups

---

*See Charles Silberman, *Crisis in the Classroom*, New York: Random House, 1970

(particularly among African Americans) to this imposition is to resist, although most time unsuccessfully, its pervasive consequence, which is culminated in the complexes of the negative self-concept syndrome (James Banks and Jean Grambs, 1971 and 1972).

In brief it could be said that equal accessibility to elaborated codes is discouraged or not encouraged. It should be noted that in the middle and secondary levels of the public school in America the presentation of English is determined by whether the student opts for, or is "advised by counselors" to pursue a vocational (skilled labor) or professional career. Of course family background and local environment will indeed shape the individual's orientation and the system's motives towards either of these two types of occupation. This however is not to say that all public school pupils in coal mining communities will be enrolled in general studies courses "as a result of their aptitude test scores," and later become coal miners, although most will. Some will make high scores and will be enrolled in college preparatory courses and will later become members of the civil superstructure: doctors, lawyers, news reporters, teachers, etc.

The most important thing is not language itself but the value placed upon occupations which have their built-in expected capacity of communication competence. Language is therefore connected to the problem of false consciousness in the division of labor. It is not only that standard varieties are more elaborate than "nonstandards" but rather that the standard varieties of English, for example, are better than the so-called "nonstandards" of English because the first is used by doctors and the second by coal miners. This is a rather pro-bourgeois formulation.

As a result of Western imperialism and the nature of the dialectic of the colonial and hierarchically stratified economy of Anglophone African countries, to be specific, English language, via Western education, flourished under conditions of extreme class polarity.

To understand the symbolic and material significance of language in the relationship between the conqueror and the conquered, which is historically the relationship between Africans and the West, we must first recognize that language is a basic and necessary component of any culture. The English revere their language and the measure of its widespread use is the measure of British superiority and imperialism. Even before the British firmly settled in Africa, the English conquest of India gave impetus to Britain's aura of cultural superiority. While all of India's successive intruders (the Turks, the Persians and the Russians) succumbed to Hinduization. *"the British were the first conquerors superior and, therefore, inaccessible to Hindu civilization,"* (Moore, p. 21 quoting from Marx and Engels *On Colonialism*, pp. 68-69). *"England [had] to fulfill a double mission in India: one destructive, the other regenerating—the annihilation of old Asiatic society, and the laying of the material foundation of Western society in Asia."* It is against this background that the English people and the English language pushed onward in Africa, although the tactics of the British were not exactly the same in Africa as in India. (Ibid.)

Twenty-seven years ago, when newly independent African countries which had inherited colonial languages entered the United Nations, speakers of English were an estimated one to one—nonnative users to native users (Mazrui, p. 82). Africans regard the English language as most desirable for modernity. Needless to say the English language is a factor of continued dependency in the present neocolonial design perpetuated by "quick capitalists." To some people 27 years ago and even now, colonial languages were perceived as alternatives to indigenous languages which celebrated the die-hard ancestral ways. Yet if a seemingly progressive nationalist movement sought to develop some indigenous African languages to accommodate the desire for modernity and go on to implement them as official languages (which may be a move toward liberation) this would not automatically eliminate the continuation of capitalist exploitation nor rule out social divisiveness in African countries. To say that updated versions of indigenous languages would resolve the problem of imperialism and social divisiveness in Africa is to exaggerate the importance of language over the framework of bourgeois nationalism, and to ignore that the diversified linguistic terrains of African countries are saturated with ethnic and micro-ethnic sentiments— symbolic forces not easily overcome by material changes. Superstructure and base are constantly feeding one another (superstructure $\rightleftharpoons$ base). In analysis, they are mutually independent and mutually inseparable at the same time.

Colonial languages like English had achieved international "trade" value (that is, cultural and capital significance in the international export market) long before the dawn of African independence, and the young nations of Africa, as economic entities and consumers of modern culture and commodities, could not easily dismiss the importance of English as well as French and Portuguese. The consequence of Africa's dependency upon world capitalism and Western world languages is the tendency to be more concerned about continued collaboration with the native user: the industrialists, the financiers and the state functionaries of the global socio-politico-economic system, and less concerned about developing the massive human resources of African countries. Again a pro-bourgeois formulation, for we are primarily dealing with the native users of the imperialist superruling class and the upper crust of the African class structure: bureaucrats, academics, politicians, compradors, plantation owners, and the like. This is not an uncommon relationship in the hegemonious structure of world capitalism.

The nationalist movements of some Third World and African countries have attempted to install indigenous languages in an effort to foster cultural autonomy and development.

When the independent governments of Indonesia, Malaysia, Tanzania and Somalia installed indigenous languages, Bahasa, Malay, Swahili* and Somali respectively (complete with orthography) to serve as national and official languages of their constituencies, the national bourgeoisie of these countries who had distinguished themselves as a privileged group were linguistically brought to the level of the masses. As one can imagine, the installation of indigenous languages as official communication media of politics, education and domestic commerce in these multilingual and multicultural societies was certainly not an easy task, but an evolutionary and (on the sociolinguistic front) a revolutionary one. The colonial languages of these countries have not been totally removed from the social, political and economic scene, but efforts are being made (through education) to introduce the new official indigenous languages, in their desired form, to the younger generations who in the future will use them exclusively.

One of the problems facing most of these countries, if not all of

---

*These three languages have been labeled non-natural and pidgin-Creoles, and were initially languages of commerce.

them, is the question of ethnolingualism and ethnic divisiveness.* Thus the official utilization of Bahasa, Malay, Swahili and Somali, each of which have a history as partial linqua francas, faces the problem of properly installing, standardizing and modernizing their orthographies, etc., which means that the respective societies to which these languages belong must learn their written form. The number of people who speak these languages is several times the number of people who read and write them. Nevertheless, the question of ethnolingualism is so pervasive in Africa and Asia that it constitutes the number one problem facing the official utilization of ethnic tongues.

Contrary to Mazrui's view that there is less linguistic nationalism generally in Africa than has been observable in Asia (p. 102), the hot debates over Hausa, Igbo and Yoruba in Nigeria and the unpublicized resistance of some Ethiopian nationalities against Amharic is evidence (and only the tip of the iceberg) of ethnolingualism and linguistic nationalism in Africa. Although we understand that: "The African situation is characterized by an expanding utilization of English and French. . ." (Ibid), the problem of linguistic nationalism accompanied by the bourgeois notion of these superposed languages as prestige symbols and as cultural capital, is at the heart of their continued expansion. As Mazrui himself puts it: "The remarkable thing is that English [like French] has not been rejected as a symbol of colonialism; it has rather been adopted as a politically neutral language beyond the reproaches of tribalism." (Ibid)

In contradistinction to the radical moves made by Indonesia, Malaysia, Tanzania and Somalia, Nigeria's solution to its multilingual and multicultural predicament (in objective reality) is the erection of the English language as the official language of education (after the first few years of primary school), of politics (until adequate arrangements are made to utilize Hausa, Igbo and Yoruba—the

---

*We recommend J.A. Fishman, "A systematization of the Whorfian hypothesis," which explains ethnolingualism as well as the history, early conclusions and development of ethnolinguistics as a scientific (but controversial) discipline. In this respect Fishman revisits the early propositions of Wilhelm Von Humbolt (1848) and traces them to Whorf. In J.W. Berry and P.R. Dasen, *Culture and Cognition: Readings in Cross-Cultural Psychology*, London: Methuen Co. Ltd., 1974, pp. 61-85.

languages of the dominant political parties) and of commerce. Given this resolution, let us examine, politically, the status of English in Nigeria from the point of view of a class analysis. In this view we shall consider 1). the policies put forward by the government making specific reference to the role of language in the country and 2) the socioeconomic character of the policymakers of Nigeria. In dealing with the latter we shall also deal with the phenomenon of Western education in Africa and the corollary appropriation of cultural capital, or as put by others, Western education as cultural imperialism. As best we can, we will attempt to explain the government disposition toward English as well as the indigenous languages of Nigeria. The concept of appropriation of surplus will become important as we examine English language in the realm of Nigeria's political economy.

The three main statements of the Federal Government's (military and civilian) policy on the role of English and Nigerian languages in the life of the nation are as follows:

The first statement is taken from the *National Policy on Education* (1977, sec. 1, para. 8) set forth by the military administration; the policy reads:

> In addition to appreciating the importance of a language in the educational process and as a means of preserving the people's culture, the Government considers it to be in the interest of national unity that each child should be encouraged to learn one of the three major languages other than his own mother-tongue. In this connection the Government considers the three major languages in Nigeria to be Hausa, Igbo and Yoruba. (Afolayan, p. 4)

The second statement was put forth by the Constitution Drafting Committee (1976) and arose from the question of selecting indigenous languages for official utilization. The committee recommended that:

> The business of the National Assembly shall be conducted in English language or such other Nigerian languages as the National Assembly may by resolution decide. (Ibid, p. 5)

The reference to Nigerian languages was later deleted by the

Constituent Assembly, but this was followed by a declaration of the Supreme Military Council (Ibid), which included in the *Constitution of the Nigerian Republic 1979* the following provision:

> The business of the National Assembly shall be conducted in English language, Hausa, Igbo and Yoruba when adequate arrangements have been made therefore. (Ibid)

There are two ideological positions in the first quotation from the Federal Republic of Nigeria's *National Policy on Education.* (Ibid, p. 4) The ideologized positions rest on indigenous Nigerian languages being "the cornerstone for national unity and meaningful education." (Ibid) The quote from the *National Policy on Education* and the final constitutional provision hold the same ideologized position, that is, ". . . national unity, development and prestige cannot be divorced from the use of indigenous languages. . . " (Ibid, p. 5) What this proves is that one, on paper the Nigerian military regime was indeed committed to an ideology of a sort, and two, their ideological influence is manifest in the present constitution. (Ibid)

The truth of the matter, though, is that the Nigerian government policy makers and their allied custodial agents are hypocritical on the question of language, particularly indigenous ones. Their opportunism only serves to appease nationalistic inclinations and to arouse endless controversy, while other matters of objective material circumstances continue to be pursued through the medium of English language and through collusion between themselves and the imperialist superstructure. With all its nationalist rhetoric of multicultural and multilingual dimensions, Nigeria is still not an Indonesia or a Somalia when it comes to practically and radically addressing the question of multilingual development in the country. Because the politico-economic life of Nigeria is locked in the clutches of transnational monopoly capitalism, and because the society manifests a class system as a result of the pyramidal and hierarchical character of its inherited colonial superstructure and production relationships, combined with a private enterprise philosophy and praxis (guided by the idea of every man for himself), it seems that the English language is entrenched in the process of assuring limited access to the available capital surplus.

After looking at the earlier quoted policies on the role of languages in Nigeria and specifically the role of indigenous languages, we should bear in mind that no arrangements have been made to install indigenous languages in the mainstream of education or politics with the exception of limited mother-tongue teaching in primary schools. No indigenous Nigerian language is taught outside its natural social domain, and little consideration is given to Nigerian pidgins. This articulates a power relationship.

As a result of a recommendation from its Mass Literacy Committee (established March 1980) the Kaduna State government (civilian) created a Mass Literacy Agency which had as one of its functions the task of enabling the entire *adult* population of Kaduna State: "to read fluently and write clearly in the Hausa language, and any other language which the Government from time-to-time may specify." It should be noted that Hausa is traditionally a superposed language vis-à-vis non-Hausa communities in northern Nigeria. At the time, Oyo State, which had embarked upon a Six Year Primary School Project with Yoruba as the medium of instruction, was leading the country in the concern for mother-tongue teaching. Both Hausa and Yoruba enjoy widespread speech communities of native users which extend beyond the boundaries of the Nigerian Republic.

Let us examine mother-tongue teaching and the role of English in relation to the Federal Government's policy on education, and on the state level with specific reference to Oyo State.

The 1977 *Federal Republic of Nigeria National Policy on Education* (para. 15/4) makes the following provision:

> Government will see to it that the medium of instruction in the primary school is initially the mother-tongue or the language of the immediate community and at a later stage, English.

More specifically the *Primary School Syllabus* of Oyo State states that:

> It is the present policy and practice for Yoruba to be used as the medium of instruction in the first three years of Primary School in the state. *During those years English is taught as a subject. After the third year English becomes the medium of instruction.* It is

envisaged however that the day will come when Yoruba will be the medium of instruction throughout the Primary School with English taught as a subject so that *it [English] can adequately perform the role of the medium of instruction in post-primary education.* (p. 3, emphasis mine)

Although the Six Year Primary School Project has pushed the Oyo State Government closer to mother-tongue teaching throughout primary school, and despite the probability that other states will follow its example (if the new military government does not intervene), we will discuss the current role of English in Education (as stated in the above policies) from a political and class point of view, thus showing a concern for socioeconomic development in a comprador (peripheral capitalist) economy. While dealing with education we shall not limit ourselves to any one level.

Judging from the italicized portions of the last quotation above, and from the second and third quotations of the Federal Government's policies referred to earlier, it is clear that English plays no small role in the educational life and politico-socialization of Nigerians, especially among those who qualitatively and quantitatively have privileged access to the cultural institutions (or cultural capital) of the modern status quo. Understanding that after the first few years of primary school English becomes the medium of instruction, and even recognizing that Yoruba will one day be installed as the medium of instruction throughout the primary level, it is clear that the rest of a student's educational life (that is, the post primary and post secondary levels)*, still requires the mastery of English which then functions solely as the medium of presentation. English, therefore, can be classified as a dominate form.

Throughout the whole education process English is a prestige marker, and serves as a cog in the machinery of bourgeois reproduction and domination. The distribution of its educational responsibility is twice that of indigenous languages by the time a student completes university.

---

*In contradistinction: "Experiments in providing university education in Malay (in Malaysia) are certainly under way." (Mazrui, p. 101)

In Nigeria English language and Western education as symbolic systems of colonialism and neocolonialism have undermined their indigenous counterparts, giving them only a narrow participation at the upper rungs of the Nigerian social hierarchy where the political and economic veins of the society are infused with particular interest.

There is indeed well-known historical evidence which accounts for the role of Western education (which gives English its importance in anglophone African as it does French in francophone territories and Portuguese in lusophone countries) in the formation of social classes in Nigeria, and as many have observed: *"One of the effects of the class system is to limit access to elaborated codes."* (Berstein, p. 105) In the history of Nigeria the idea, and indeed the concrete reality of limited access to elaborated codes is seen in the limited accessibility to status quo Nigerian English which is determined by sociocultural, sociolinguistic and socio-politico-economic factors. As best we can, we will attempt to briefly explain the sociocultural, sociolinguistic and material factors which account for limited access to English in Nigeria. Admittedly, the following historical account is sketchy and somewhat inadequate to any Nigerian historian.

First of all Nigerians do not by origin belong to the English speaking community—and if linguistic intuition is of critical importance to communication competence and performance, and if this intuitive capacity is for the most part peculiar to mother-tongue speakers (or at least more easily exercised among them), then it seems to follow that in Nigeria the question of access to status quo English is even more complex than it may appear to be in purely sociopolitical terms. This does not, however, imply that a desirable competence in and performance of a second language is unattainable; linguistic competence and performance are relative. We assume, though, from observation that the cultural environment which aids the development of an intuitive capacity for using the English language is not accessible to the masses of Nigeria. We should also point out that the question of intuitive capacity would still be present if any single natural indigenous language was superposed on the entire Nigerian public which we know to have a multilingual face.

Nevertheless the socio-politico-economic motives which support limited access to a status quo English in Nigeria are quite impressive, with a long history dating back to the "civilizing" period of the 19th century when the British missionaries (anti-slavery abolitionists) brought to West Africa Christianity and introduced Western education in the medium of English language.

The capital motive behind the abolitionist movement and civilizing missions in West Africa rests in the proposition that the African interior was an untapped and necessary source of raw materials for the industrial and commercial sector of England. In order to enhance the growth of the industrial mode of production and in order to promote civilization, British industrialists and merchants were encouraged to invest in the "development" of Africa so as to create a new system of trade that would replace the slave trade. This was basically the vision of the abolitionist leader T.F. Buxton and the purpose of the 1941 Niger expedition (among which we find Rev. Samuel Adjai Crowther, an England-educated Yoruba). (Carnoy, p. 126-128 and Fage, p. 129) It was envisioned: "The new trade must be free. It must produce both a free peasantry and a new commercial and industrial class." (Carnoy, Ibid)

The English speaking missions (as one representative of several imperial forces) who first installed the English language in Africa are historically important to an understanding of how modern capitalist philosophy and life style was introduced and inculcated in the social consciousness of Africans. What should be noted first is: "Missionary work in Africa and the schools connected with the missions were . . . born of a civilizing purpose, a purpose that not only involved religious conversion but the acceptance of new economic and social organizations." (Carnoy, p. 128) The ultimate aim of the antislavery movement in West Africa, including Nigeria, was "to convert Africans into palm oil and cocoa producers [and therefore] Europeans had to bring the ['advantages'] of 'legitimate' trade to Africans." (Ibid, p. 123) In the long run Western education, in this case under the British, played a significant role in accommodating this end by creating a buffer group, however modest at first, of educated Nigerian speakers of English who would protect the collaborated interest of the colonialist and their indigenous agents.

"After the Niger expedition and after the British merchants and navy had been operating along the coast and in the Niger delta for some time, the first English speaking missionaries began to arrive in Southern Nigeria." (Ibid, p. 127) First Thomas Birch Freeman and

Henry Townsend arrived at Badagry in 1842 and in 1846 were followed by the Church of Scotland Mission under Reverend Hope Waddell who started the settlement at Calabar. Missions were also set up in Abeokuta where their main constituency were Sierra Leoneans and Africans from Brazil and the Caribbean, who resettled in Nigeria in the 1840s and 1850s.*

The idealism of early capitalism is very much present in the writing of this period as well as in the genetic theories of the European erudite community which along with Christianity gave morality to imperialism. The idealism of capitalism fostered the notion that great value should be placed on the profitability of production, with the view of changing African's life style so as to become like the Europeans in order to "benefit from" or "appreciate" the high economic returns. Since among Africans there existed a modest demand for academic education, for the most part this was achieved.

When political annexation began to shape new relationships between the colonialist and the people of Nigeria, missionaries lost much of their foothold in the country. The colonial administration was more concerned about politics and commerce and less concerned about civilizing missions—notwithstanding the fact that Western education brought by the English missionaries had already broken the ground for breeding an indigenous buffer group to help administer (with minimal responsibilities prior to 1952, as compared to the collaborating traditional rulers) and support the political and commercial interest of the colony.

Rather than create the wrong impression about the limited demand for and impact of Western education (and the limited demand of

---

*The African American Harvard educated physician, Martin Delaney also took an interest in settlements in Nigeria and in 1858 signed a treaty with eight kings on behalf of Africans in America (represented by the Niger Valley Exploring Party) granting the right and privilege to African American to resettle in unoccupied areas of Abeokuta. Notwithstanding Delaney's courageous abolitionist background and his prominence as a pioneer of Pan-Africanism, the Niger Valley Exploring Party to which he belonged was as well a civilizing imperial force with economic interest which was influenced by early American capitalism. (Ofari, p. 20) The Niger Valley group falls in line with Buxton's suggestion that, ". . . the government (of Britain) and merchants should rely on Africans from Sierra Leone and the Americans as their agents." (Carnoy, p. 127).

indigenes complemented the limited need of the colonialist for a buffer group), let us observe the chart below giving an account of the percentage of enrollment of the school age population in Provinces of Southern Nigeria in 1921 and 1931, eight decades after the Niger Expedition:

Province	1921	1931
Western Region:		
Lagos and Colony	28.4	39.5
Abeokuta	6.3	7.4
Benin	4.0	10.3
Ijebu	16.7	13.0 decline
Ondo	4.8	7.3
Oyo	2.3	4.4
Warri	6.2	10.4
Eastern Region:		
Calabar	20.4	30.2
Ogoja	2.3	1.5 decline
Onitsha	9.3	11.8
Owerri	5.5	13.5
British Cameroons	1.8	10.4
All Provinces	9.2	12.5

(Source: David Abernethy, *Political Dilemma of Popular Education,* Stanford: Standford University Press, 1969, p. 37 in Carnoy, p. 134)

The percentage of enrollment of the school age population in Lagos, Calabar and Ijebu needs some explanation. Besides the fact that missionaries arrived in Lagos and Calabar much earlier than in other areas of Nigeria, these two provinces were the commercial and administrative centers of the west and east respectively and therefore demanded an educated indigenous buffer group to make up the general (rank and file) administrative staff. We should recall that according to the Clifford Constitution arrangements of 1922 there were only four elected indigenous representatives, and three were from Lagos and one was from Calabar. There were no elected representatives from the north and, in fact, other indigenes brought into the arrangement were nominated by the colonial authorities.

As for Ijebu, its comparatively high percentage of enrollment can be traced back to the collapse of the Ijebu resistance against the British. In spite of the fact that Ijebus had long used firearms (acquired through trade) and in spite of the fact that Ijebus outnumbered the British opposition in 1892, the British overwhelmingly defeated them and their collective concept of military superiority was shattered. As a result of this demoralization the Ijebus had to seek a new identity and world view. What made the Ijebus so important to the colonial authorities in Lagos was their strategic location and history as an entity which had traditionally controlled trade between Lagos and the hinterland. The Ijebus' need for a new identity and the imperialist interest in expanding their enterprise led to the development of the English speaking educated class of the Ijebus. The first missionary school was established in Ijebu in 1893, shortly after the 1892 battle.

The decline in the Ijebu school age enrollment (1931) has much to do with the immigration of educated Ijebus of previous generations who sought employment in various arms of the colonial civil service and in the private sector. Indeed many went to Lagos.

One might imagine that Benin, Warri, and Onitsha would also be major centers of commerce, administration and education, the first being near to the coast, the second being a coastal town and the third being located on the Niger River water route. However, these provinces were not in the mainstream of colonial affairs during the pre-World War II period.

Prior to the post-World War II period the small number of missionary and federal college trained Nigerians and the smaller number of Nigerians who trained in universities abroad (the latter were the eligible academics who participated in influential debating societies in Europe) did not constitute an indigenous "power" elite. The Sierra Leonean, Brazilian, and West Indian extraction, the traditional leaders, the indigenous businessmen and the national liberation leaders did not control the decision-making apparatus in any significant way. The colonial administrators constituted the real ruling class in Nigeria; they alone controlled state power and access to it. (Osoba, p. 2) Even the emirates in the north who by virtue of the Islamic life style were less affected by missions and the secular type

Western education provided there, succumbed to the policy objectives and goals of the colonial administration.

When representative and Majority African Rule on an elective basis was introduced, Western educated Nigerians (who had formerly been comparatively the lesser important indigenous agents of the colonial administration) began to exercise more authority, even to the extent that old traditional leaders were peripheralized vis-à-vis the political mainstream of the south. In the period from 1945 to 1952 the spirit of African Nationalism had, in concrete terms on the continent, and in symbolic terms at the 1945 Fifth Pan-African Congress in Manchester England, made it clear to the West that a new arrangement of imperialist rule and the co-opting of the African nationalist spirit was necessary. This foreseen new arrangement was self-imposed on European and American leaders who called for the right to self-determination for all nations after the Second World War. Thus the small indigenous Western-educated buffer group which had been in the pipe line for several decades possessed the potential (by virtue of their cultural capital) to serve as custodians of post-World War imperialism. Having already taken advantage of the cultural capital of traditional colonialism this bilingual and bicultural sector of the Nigerian population went ahead and seized the opportunity to benefit from the surplus capital of neocolonialism and hurled themselves into the echelons of politics and economic affairs. As elected officials after 1952 and as free-enterprise entrepreneurs they monopolized all domestic power. According to Osoba:

> Perhaps the most significant factor ... was their attitude to the economic development of Nigeria on a capitalist free-enterprise basis and the way in which individual members ... (even those who were bureaucrats in the Native Authorities of the emirates before being elected to Kaduna or Lagos) showed keen interest in business and the acquisition of capital. It would be interesting to compute, although understandably there would be no reliable data, the percentage of members of regional and federal legislatures and executives from 1952 to 1965 who did not dabble at all in business: my guess [says Osoba] is that it would be very low indeed. The most reliable measure, however, of the general involvement of members of the Nigeria power elite in business is the enthusiasm

with which all the governments in Nigeria . . . created optional conditions for the operation of private capital, whether foreign or domestic. (p. 9)

When we look, from 1952—onward, at the economic program of the Western-educated Nigerian, who monopolized the internationally accepted variety of English, we then realize the boundless and unscrupulous efforts of this group to "advance" themselves to the level of a neocolonial bourgeoisie. The Nigerian "bourgeoisie" is a *"lumpen-bourgeoisie"* in as much as it does not own or control industrial production (a fundamental characteristic of real capitalism); this role belongs to Western imperialists. The Nigerian "bourgeoisie" are merely middlemen-contractors, dependent manufacturers, wholesalers and retailers, planters and administrators, professionals and academics, who benefit, some less than others, from the surplus capital of the national product. Nevertheless they are a capital-owning class.

Osoba refers to two economists S.P. Schatz and S.I. Edokpayi (1962) who made the following empirically-supported observation:

A FUNDAMENTAL feature of Nigerian economic policy is the effort to develop the economy by encouraging Nigerian private enterprise. To this end the Regional and Federal Governments have devised many programs, such as tax relief of various kinds, technical and managerial advice and assistance, industrial estates, government patronage, the provision of credit, and many others. (p. 11).

Osoba also points out that on the level of praxis this Nigerian economic policy did not follow the indiscriminate promotion of indigenous private enterprise, on the contrary the allocation of government business aid was done in an essentially discriminatory manner, and in this respect benefited those in the hierarchy of the existing political parties—Action Group, Northern People's Congress (N.P.C.) and National Council of Nigeria and the Cameroons (NCNC).* (Ibid) These beneficiaries, as can be guessed, were mostly

---

*Later became the National Council of Nigerian Citizens.

Western educated, most had completed teacher training colleges, held professional certificates or attended university abroad.

Since the neocolonial program inherited the English language as the language of all its official endeavors and deemed it a valuable import item, and since it transplanted the basic superstructures of Western capitalist culture, which needed academic and professional trained custodians, the larger portion of the Nigerian population was definitely outside the mainstream of domestic and international affairs, leaving the front and back doors wide open for exploitation and bribery. The inaccessibility of the sociocultural, political and economic organs of the Nigerian neocolonial state to the Nigerian masses is connected to the class dialectics of the country and the continued poverty of its people.

Those belonging to the 1930s baby crop of mission or federal college trained Nigerians became the first group of specialists of considerable size (although still comparatively small). Many of them schooled at prestigious federal colleges in the country, and took University of London degrees from the University College at Ibadan, which can be regarded as the English's academic Ivory Tower of West Africa. The real luxury of Western-English style education lies in the fact that those who possess this cultural capital constitute a significant number of those who took their profits and developed their businesses from the surplus capital of cocoa, ground nuts and palm oil which produced 60 percent of the national wealth prior to the 1970s.

It is also interesting that the indigenous elites of the 1950s accepted the 50/50 oil deal offered to Nigeria in 1959 by Shell British Petroleum Company, ten years before the real oil boom. This bit of historical information, just goes to show the extreme business enthusiasm of the period. The same 50/50 oil deal met hostile resistance in the Arab world and even led to what we now know as OPEC. The 50/50 agreement between Shell BP and the Nigerian "bourgeoisie" was honored until Nigeria joined the OPEC bloc after the civil war.

The oil boom, which followed the Nigerian civil war, and is considered to be a material motive thereof, gave rise to a second set of bourgeoisified Nigerians who followed the example of the old stock. The "bourgeoisie" (the cline between class groups notwithstanding) during this period comprised the surviving university trained heroes of the independence movement who acquired their profits through banking, professional enterprise and cocoa trade, etc., the oil boom tycoons and the formally trained military top brass who make up the 1930s baby crop, and top jurists, government and private executives, political leaders and academicians (respectively, Obafemi Awolowo, Nnamdi Azikiwe, Waziri Ibrahim; Joseph Wayas, T.O.S. Benson, A.O. Saraki, R.O.A. Akinjide, Fatai Williams, etc.).

The surplus capital of the oil boom period attracted all types of imperialist investors looking for new deals which gave rise to several instant capitalists (e.g., M.O.K. Abiola).

What is important to bear in mind throughout our discussion is how the biculturality and the bilinguality, inculcated through Western education, qualified the Nigerian upper class to manipulate the flow of capital in the country. It is interesting that the same Western education that provided Western egalitarian ideals which enhanced the independence struggle, is the same Western education which has more devastatingly encouraged capitalist values and the formation of a comprador economy. Now looking at the present period let us examine the accessibility or inaccessibility of Euro-cultural capital vis-à-vis the Nigerian populace. While doing this we shall also look at the strategies of Western education as an agent of imperialism, with a brief reference to Latin America.

In spite of the popularization of primary and secondary education, and post secondary school relief in the western UPN* controlled part of Nigeria (1979-1983), which actually proved to be more or less a symbolic political play of so-called populist politicians, the truth is that the kind of formal education (that is specialized university training) required to belong to the upper echelon of capital owners is hardly obtainable. And though we may still find non-university trained elements from the 1930s baby crop in the present ruling class, we speculate that this will not persist with future generations. Obviously this is not simply because a foreign and imperial language was made an official and second language of the society and as such ostracizes the majority of Nigerians from the bicultural-bilingual and politico-economic mainstream of this modern society, but also because capitalism, which is the economic philosophy and practice of

---

*Unity Party of Nigeria.

the civil superstructure, historically does not permit equal access to symbolic or material capital, for if it did so it would not be capitalism. Although it is possible for the industrial production of many Western monolingual countries to provide adequate and efficient educational systems, the accessibility to cultural capital, or shall we say the dissemination of knowledge, is still limited under the Western class system (European and American). Bernstein's observation of the sociolinguistic nature (code differentiation) of Western monolingual societies speaks to this:

> The class system has deeply marked the distribution within society. It has given differential access to the sense that the world is permeable. It has sealed off communities from each other and has ranked these communities on a scale of invidious insulation. It would be a little naive to believe that difference in knowledge, difference in the sense of the possible, combined with invidious insulation, rooted in differential *material* well-being, would not affect the forms of different social classes.
>
> We can see that the class system has affected the distribution of knowledge. Historically, and now, only a tiny percentage of the population has been socialized into knowledge at the level of meta-languages of control and innovation, whereas the mass of the population has been socialized into knowledge at the level of context-tied operations. (p. 104)

Although the same implications of cross-class bias, mentioned earlier in this discussion (that is, the lower class is wanting in innovation and their language is "context-tied"), underlay Bernstein's observations, he recognizes the invidious inequality of the distribution of knowledge, as cultural capital, in the class system.

Western capitalism has introduced and continues to introduce its system of class stratified education to the underdeveloped clients of imperialism. This is specifically the case in Latin America (others notwithstanding).

The comprehensive high school, a 19th century "U.S. high school expansion" phenomenon, exported to Latin America from the United States, was initially designed to maintain social control and answer to the demand for differential labor needed by industries. While comprehensive high schools open their doors to all comers, from all classes, the pupils are still divided according to their *vocational aptitudes*. The imperialist engineers also export *aptitude tests* and *vocational guidance*: "the schools must select children more systematically according to their abilities and the needs of the economic system," while at the same time hide "behind a facade of democracy and equal opportunity." (Carnoy, pp. 358-359)

The process described here is commonly called the "tracking system," and has undergone several reforms and is still used in the West today. In a sense this strategy of Western bourgeois education is not in itself the problem, that is, the monitoring of individual potential is not in itself bad. However, the ideology, the invidious insulation and the material basis which informs such strategy is actually the target of our contention. Thus much controversy has arisen with regard to aptitude tests, which determine the vocational direction of pupils subjected to this strategy. The most recurrent accusation is that these aptitude tests are socially and culturally biased against non-mainstream and/or non-Europeanized members of school aged publics. Our contention is that the tracking system in bourgeois education perpetuates quasi-caste formations.

Now coming to Nigeria, its educational system in a historical review is divided into Government schools, private mission schools, military schools, and private secular schools. Let us first discuss the mission schools, the militay schools and the private secular schools.

Being at first private institutons, the mission schools were fully responsible for their overhead and therefore their fees were high. Since they were the first schools set up in the country, mission schools for a long time built up a reputation of prestige for both moral and academic reasons. Their clients were primarily children of the upper class, with some patronized students from the lower class. The mission schools offered primary and secondary education, and basically accommodated the mutual religious faith of its constituency and often converted nondenomination recruits. As a result of state policy objectives, most of these schools died off after producing several generations of upper-class Nigerians during colonial rule.

The military schools are *naturally* exclusive. They provide primary education to the children of Army, Navy and Air Force personnel.

The children of the military top brass who attend these schools usually pass on to expensive Federal Government high schools and higher schools.

The private secular schools, nonreligious types, are recent, relatively expensive and few in number. They cater to the primary school age children of professionals and well-to-do citizens. So-called private secular secondary schools which were actually recipients of state grants (except for International School, Ibadan which received such grants through the University of Ibadan and obtained additional funds from the Rockefeller Foundation) and were always supported by the locale, the rightful owners, have been absorbed by the state. This move (state take-over) caused a few "private education" activists, like Michael Enyia (formerly at the University of Michigan) to pursue their educationalist endeavors outside the country.

What we have described above are educational institutions which are either "naturally" exclusive, or voluntarily exclusive as a result of material and "spiritual" (religious) considerations. The next category, the government schools, cross all the levels of education, state primary schools, state and federal secondary and higher schools and federal universities. Government schools are similar to the former types (that is, there are some restrictions), but in a symbolic sense are still different. Their doors are open to all comers: they are quasi-democratic. Although they are supposed to represent government (state and federal) accountability to the masses, they still exist outside the material reality (possibility) of lower-class wage earners and peasants. Since the schooling of lower-class Nigerian children competes with the demand for child labor in the home (this is a matter of subsistence), many who start school, and continue for a while, eventually drop out before reaching the secondary level. This is a general problem from the beginning, the boarding expense of some state and federal colleges notwithstanding.

The school age constituency of government schools comprise the children of elites, top military officers, the civil service senior staff, successful entrepreneurs, and professionals; and of petty traders, civil service rank and file, some private sector wage earners, and well-to-do peasants—some of whom are understandably patronized.

While in western Nigeria the question of costly education has long been a concern of politicians and educationalists who have implemented a free public education scheme to remedy the problem of "possibility," and increase the school age enrollment, the *secret confessions* about schooling expenses in this region still persist. (These are expenses for books, supplies, repairs, etc.) It is our guess that state bursaries aimed at financially aiding university students, and salaries take (or took) a great chunk of the western states' educational budgets. When we consider government accountability to mass education we must recognize that most of the national budget is appropriated to contractors, who seek quick profits and render inefficient services.

Across the board all Nigerian pupils pass through the various steps (classes and levels) of the educational system according to merit and material circumstance. The ability of students to pass costly imported tests from Britain, and the privilege of capital ownership, are *a priori* determinants of occupational direction. The invidious competitive sociology within each category of Nigerian schools, combined with the invidious competitive relationship between them, is one symptom of class stratification in education and society.

The accumulative cost alone of university academic training in Nigeria is far above the income of the general populace, who cannot afford the prestige life style of the university environment. The expansion of university education is faced with a shortage of facilities and academic staff. Besides the fact that they are citadel manufacturers of cultural capital, the universities manifest a class system within their authoritarian hierarchical structure inherited from the old colonial system, in spite of indigenous reforms. Indeed the 1978 student crisis, the 1980 Academic Union strike, the 1981 "Junior" staff strike, combined with some obscure *contracted* wage labor strikes, and the 1981 University of Lagos Crisis, plus other examples of hierarchy infighting, clearly characterize the divisive antagonism behind the veil of university prestige. Doubtless these are features of a class system in a neocolonial state.

The importance of all the facts and observations stated so far is inescapable; there is something about the Nigerian educational system that dims one's sense of possibility; and like all Western manufactured imports of control and consumption, Nigeria's Western styled educational system distorts human purpose. In the final analysis, only revolutionary and liberating steps at all levels of the society can eradicate the ostracism of the masses by the societal control towers.

Nevertheless, when we look back at the question of the distribution of cultural capital, the need for a mutually accessible medium (or media) of communication at all levels, language and education are evidently recognized as means to inclusion by the policy makers of Nigeria, who appear, at least at the level of rhetoric, to be sensitive to the multicultural and multilingual development of the society.

The problems which face a proper implementation of a multicultural and multilingual program (and which force English on the society as a "unifying" agent) are primarily moral, academic and administrative (notwithstanding class interests), and can only be overcome over a very long period.

The moral problem exists in the Nigerian people, in all classes, in each linguistic community, and in each individual. This is the problem of rejecting things that are indigenously derived but are not of the cultural reality of the immediate community—not of the self. This is the problem of multinationality (ethnic nationalism), which contributes to the second problem of academic dimensions.

On the academic level Nigeria has not found it possible to offer any of the major indigenous languages outside their sociolinguistic territories, and this takes us back to the moral question and beyond. It is our guess that the present generation of Nigerian educators and students (like the general populace) are not willing to learn any indigenous language other than their mother-tongue, and would not be enthusiastic about teaching their mother-tongue outside its domain though we hope this will soon change. Beyond the moral question facing academics, there is a shortage of indigenous language teachers and the same is true of competent English language teachers as well. In addition, not enough expert attention has been paid to the (modern) development of indigenous languages in the areas of science and technology. Although Government administration policy encourages multicultural and multilingual development, their preoccupation seems to be the biculturalism and bilingualism (which foster limited access) of the status quo. Little care has been taken to assure the success of multicultural and multilingual development—this issue appears to be too hot to handle. Much of what is done in this direction is the work of a handful of innovative intellectuals who sometimes get lucky enough to capture the attention of the government. We have observed that in areas of Nigeria where either an indigenous language does not compete with other native tongues or where an indigenous language is superposed on others, language specialists would prefer to ignore pidgin since the sociolinguistic terrain in such situations does not demand the use of pidgin. The attitude which underlies this thinking disregards the national and universal accountability of academia. It even ignores the pedagogical strategy of using pidgin as a spring-board to the desired standard usage of English, an approach which is an important contribution to mid-western and eastern Nigeria where pidgin is a lingua franca. Seeing the *import* of any Nigerian language in the narrow confines of regionalism will not carry the country very far along the path of multilingual development. It is my guess that more Nigerians use pidgin than not. Pidgin deserves consideration for development and adoption as a national and official language.

Before moving on to the next point we would like to draw attention to the fact that attitudes which manifest narrow-minded regionalism or *statism*, (in a class system), attitudes wanting a dialectical and critical awareness, have accommodated the ambitions of bourgeois elements who in many conspicuous and inconspicuous ways encourage divisiveness and form their political base on the disparities of it. The history of Nigeria has shown that there are forces within the civil superstructure which use political power as a means to profit. Although we recognize that, in theory, the state is a midwife of government accountability, statism, like regionalism, has played a decisive role in the formation of the "bourgeoisie" and in the further entrenchment of bourgeois political economy.

We agree that if each Nigerian child "and worker" is made literate in his mother-tongue and in English, and if he or she learns one of the three major tongues, (other than the mother-tongue, if it is a major language), it is possible that one day Nigeria will be able to quantify the percentile of the users of the three major languages and decide upon a single national language of indigenous status, or, in this age of technology, even properly implement the three as official languages. This is an evolutionary process which requires building positive social relationships in the society. Above all a radical change in the manner of distribution of cultural capital (this includes English language) is the first step toward positive social development.

When we attempt to measure or even itemize the possibility of adopting a unifying medium of communication in Nigeria, we must try to recapture the spirit of the resolution passed at the Second Congress of Negro [*sic*] Writers and Artists in Rome, 1959, which expressed an even greater task for African linguists and African peoples generally. This was the question of adopting a continental language, selected by consensus from the pool of indigenous languages. But the openmindedness, the sacrifice of cultural arrogance which underlies this idealism, at this point in history when internal economic interchange is vital to the continent, is outside the realm of possibility. The Second Congress of Negro Writers and Artists passed:

1. that free and liberated black Africa should not adopt any European or other languages as a national tongue;

2. that one African language shoud be chosen . . . that all Africans would learn this national language besides their own regional language; and

3. that a team of linguists be instructed to enrich this language as rapidly as possible, with the terminology for expression of modern philosophy, science and technology. (Soyinka, p. 47)

This resolution seemingly runs counter to the ambition of any single African country to erect a national language. Nonetheless, if such wide-reaching, openminded idealism can be entertained by the cognitive constructs of language, then certainly Nigeria must be openminded enough to do whatever is necessary to adopt a unifying national language from the indigenous reservoir of Nigerian mother-tongues, (not to preclude pidgin), and make it accessible to all, regardless of class, race, sex or creed. However, given the history of Nigeria's ethnolinguistic situation and given the resistance from minority representatives in the National Assembly (of the deposed civilian regime) against the constitutional installment of Hausa, Igbo and Yoruba as national languages, this calling is probably as idealistic as the previously mentioned 1959 resolution. Again we seem to be deadlocked with English, and if this must be the case then radical arrangements need to be made to redistribute the English language as a desired cultural compulsive of modern day Nigeria. This calling demands nothing less than a radical and revolutionary material transformation: a redistribution of the national wealth, which will favor mass development over private profits and the privilege of bourgeois alienation, is in order.

Material and symbolic transformation are violent processes which Marx articulates in his 1859 Preface to the *Contribution to the Critique of Political Economy*:

> The general conclusion at which [he] arrived and which, once reached, became the guiding principle of [his] studies can be' summarized as follows. In the social production of their existence, [people] inevitably enter into definite relations, which are independent of their will, namely relations of production appropriate to a given stage in the development of their material forces of production. The totality of these relations of production constitutes the economic structure of society, the real foundation, on which arises a legal and political superstructure and to which correspond *definite [fixed] forms* of social consciousness. The mode of production of material life conditions the general process of *social, political and intellectual life*. It is not the consciousness of men that determines their existence, *but their social existence that determines their consciousness.* At a certain stage of development, the material productive forces of society come into conflict with the existing relations of production or—this merely expresses the same thing in legal terms—with the property relations within the framework of which they have operated hitherto. From forms of development of the productive forces these relations turn into their fetters. Then begins an era of social revolution. The changes in the economic foundation lead sooner or later to the transformation of the whole immense superstructure. In studying such transformations it is always necessary to distinguish between the material transformation of the economic conditions of production, which can be determined with the precision of natural science, and *the legal, political, religious, artistic or philosophic [language and education]—in short, ideological forms in which men become conscious*

of this conflict and fight it out.* Just as one does not judge an individual by what he thinks about himself, so one cannot judge such a period of transformation by its consciousness, but on the contrary, this consciousness must be explained from the contradictions of material life, from the conflict existing between the social forces of production and the relations of production. No social order is ever destroyed before all the productive forces for which it is sufficient have been developed, and new superior relations of production never replace older ones before the material conditions for their existence have matured within the framework of the old society. Mankind thus inevitably sets itself only such tasks as it is able to solve, since closer examination will always show that the problem itself arises only when the material conditions for its solution are already present or at least in the course of formation. In broad outline, the Asiatic, ancient, feudal and modern bourgeois modes of production may be designated as epochs marking progress in the economic development of society. The bourgeois mode of production is the last antagonistic form of the social process of production—antagonistic not in the sense of individual antagonism but of an antagonism that emanates from the individuals' social conditions of existence—but the productive forces developing within bourgeois society create also the material conditions for a solution of this antagonism. The prehistory of human society accordingly closes with this social formation. (pp. 20-22, emphasis mine)

Operating alongside the social relations of production and social transformation, which Marx describes, are modes of perception couched in a hegemony of relationships. These modes of perception articulate to the individual, to the group and to the class, a subjective position, in what Raymond Williams has called *a structure of feeling.*

... the actual alternative to the received and produced fixed (defined) forms is not silence: not the absence, the unconscious,

---

*Also considered in the same way of this discussion in Raymond Williams, *Marxism and Literature*, pp. 75-76.

which bourgeois culture has mythicized. It is a kind of feeling and thinking which is indeed social and material, but each in an embryonic phase before it can become fully articulate and defined exchange. Its relations with the already articulate and defined are then exceptionally complex. (Williams, p. 131)

It is after all, the observatory process (mediated by the world) and the formulation and subsequent concretization of ideas (ideology) which culminate the human spirit—the collectivization of subjective and objective views of reality—that move us through events of history. It is the subjective and objective variables, in conflict, which require us "to fight it out."

Until revolutionary changes overtake the present mode of production and the ideology which informs it, and until there is a radical change in production and social relationships, the question of invidious divisiveness in language and in education will not be resolved. Ultimately a positive transformation of the social consciousness of Nigerians is the only answer to the question of proper multilingual and multicultural development of that multinational, class stratified society—which historically has been faced with imposed bilingualism and biculturalism, which has served as an opportune advantage for those of privilege at the upper rungs of the social hierarchy.

Conclusion

It is naive and an act of blind faith to expect that popular liberation can be achieved through the custodial institutions of a bourgeois state, and for this reason we offer no strategies or blue prints for the consideration of such. If cynics hold that the very exercise of writing this essay invalidates this absence of faith then we assure that our "faith" is half-hearted. Radical writers are cultural entrepreneurs—publishing is a mode of production articulated to subsistence. In art and/or academia, radicalism and subsistence constitute a paradox of hegemonic relations. In part it is only resolved, in an alternative sense, through a value of resistance. What we can suggest along the lines of strategy is for the consideration of the brave and dialogical men and women committed to a revolutionary spirit and praxis.

Our strategy is work, a holistic approach to the dialectic of interconnected social classes. Although one's consciousness may reflect liberation, this reflection alone, without positive and active participation in the process of transformation cannot achieve the goal of liberation. Thus, work guided by single-minded prescriptions, a working relationship that denies some men the right to ideologize the world through acts of dialogue cannot achieve liberation. Responsible praxis must involve the search for a proper class analysis which recognizes historically each man's (person's) humanity (logic) and social being.

Our strategy calls for popular liberating education not education for domination and alienation. Our strategy calls for "true dialogue" and work (praxis) with the exploited and oppressed constituency in the constituent environment. This strategy calls for commitment to good will toward others and commitment to liberation as an active-generative process for collective freedom, not a mere commitment to ideology, to work for work sake, to education, to scholarship, or to sentimentality or opportunism. (Freire, pp. 50-62)

What must be borne in mind: movement is constant; the gradual and radical quantitative changes arising from the inherent contradictions of opposed and yet interconnected and interdependent class groups will bring about qualitative changes, which will be either generative acts of liberation or degenerative acts of oppression.

Bibliography

Achebe, Chinua. *Things Fall Apart*. Greenwich, Connecticut: Fawcett Publications, Inc., 1959.

Afolayan, Adebisi. "The Place of English In Nigerian Education as an Agent of Proper Multilingual and Multicultural Development." Paper delivered at English Language and Literature Workshop, Department of Adult Education, University of Ibadan, Ibadan, Nigeria, August 13-30, 1980; later expanded in a paper entitled "The English Language in Nigerian Education as an Agent of Proper Multicultural Development." Seminar Paper, Department of English Language, University of Ife, Ile-Ife, Nigeria, 5th March 1981. Both of the papers grew out of a lecture delivered to the Ifevarsity English Society, 1980.

Aronson, C. and Meo, M., Trans. *A Prospectus for Marx's Mathematical Manuscripts*. Oakland, California: Marx's Mathematical Manuscripts, 1982.

Atai, Uko. *The Beehive*. An Unpublished Play. 1981.

Baker, Houston A. *The Journey Back: Issues in Black Literature and Criticism.* Chicago: University of Chicago Press, 1980.

Banks, James and Grambs, Jean. *Black Self-Concept: Implications for Education and Social Science.* New York: McGraw-Hill Book Co., 1972.

Bernstein, Basil. "Social Class, Language and Socialization." In *Language In Education, A Source Book.* Prepared by the Language and Learning Course Team at the Open University. London: Routledge and Kegan Paul in association with The Open University Press, 1972.

Berry, Margaret. *Introduction to Systematic Linguistics.* Vol. 1 *Structures and Systems.* London: B.T. Batsford, 1975.

Beveridge, W.I.B. *The Art of Scientific Investigation.* London: Heinemann, 1950.

Bourdieu, Pierre. *Outline of a Theory of Practice.* Cambridge: Cambridge University Press, 1977.

Bruner, Jerome S. *The Relevance of Education*. Edited by Anita Gil. New York: W.W. Norton, 1973.

Carnoy, Martin. *Education as Cultural Imperialism*. New York: David McKay Co., 1974.

Cox, Oliver C. *Caste Class and Race, a Study in Social Dynamics*. New York: Monthly Review Press, 1970.

Cruse, Harold. *The Crisis of the Negro Intellectual*. New York: William Morrow and Co., 1967.

Engels, Frederick. *The Origin of the Family Private Property and the State*. Moscow: Progress Publishers, 1948.

Ervin-Tripp, Susan M. "Sociolinguistics." In *Advances in the Sociology of Language*. Vol. 1, 2nd ed. edited by Joshua A. Fishman. The Hague: Mouton, 1976.

Fage, J.D. *A History of West Africa: An Introductory Survey*. 4th ed. London: Cambridge University Press, 1969.

Fishman, J.A. (1960) "A Systematization of the Whorfian Hypothesis." In *Culture and Cognition: Reading in Cross-Cultural Psychology*, edited by J.W. Berry and P.R. Dasen. London: Methuen, 1974.

Fowler, H.W. *Modern English Language*. Oxford: Clarendon, 1975.

Freire, Paulo. *Pedagogy of the Oppressed*. Translated by Myra Bergman Ramos. Middlesex, England: Penguin Books, 1972.

Gould, L. Harry. *Marxist Glossary*. San Francisco, California: Proletarian Publishers, 1943.

Gutler, Anthony; Hieneess, Barry; Hirst, Paul and Hussain, Athar. *Marx's Capital and Capitalism Today*. Vol. I, London: Routledge and Kegan Paul, 1977.

Halliday, M.A.K. *Language as Social Semiotic, The Social Interpretation of Language and Meaning*. London: Edward Arnold Publishers, 1978.

Hegel, George W.F. *Lectures on the Philosophy of World History*. Cambridge: Cambridge University Press, 1975.

Holt, Grace Sims. "Metaphor, Black Discourse Style, and Cultural Reality." A paper presented at the Seventh Annual Southern Conference on Language Teaching, Atlanta, Georgia, October 22, 1971.

Hymes, Dell., ed. *Pidginization and Creolization of Languages.* London: Cambridge University Press, 1968.

Labov, William. "The Logic of Nonstandard English." In *The Study of Nonstandard English.* Champaign, Illinois: National Council of Teachers of English, 1970.

Larrain, Jorge. *The Concept of Ideology.* London: Hutchinson, 1979. See "Althusser's 'Structural' Conception of Ideology," pp. 154-164.

Lenin, V.I. *Imperialism, The Highest Stage of Capitalism.* Peking: Foreign Languages Press, 1973.

Lenin, V.I. *On Literature and Art.* Moscow: Progress Publishers, 1978.

Lenin, V.I. *The State.* Peking: Foreign Languages Press, 1970.

Marx, Karl. *Capital.* Vol. 1, *The Process of Production of Capital.* Translated by Samuel Moore and Edward Eveling. Edited by Frederick Engels. Moscow: Progress Publishers, 1978.

Marx, Karl. *Capital.* Vol, 3, *The Process of Capitalist Production as a Whole.* Edited by Fredrick Engels. Moscow: Progress Publishers, 1977.

Marx, Karl. (1859 Preface) *Contricultion of the Critique of Political Economy.* New York: Internation Publishers, 1970.

Mazrui, Ali A. *World Culture and the Black Experience.* The John Danz Lectures. Seattle: University of Washington Press, 1974.

Moore, Carlos. *Were Marx and Engels White Racists? The Prolet-Aryan Outlook of Marx and Engels.* Chicago: Institute of Positive Education, 1972. Moore's articulations are nativist but nonetheless relevant to a discourse on ideological imperialism.

Nigeria. Federal Ministry of Information. *The Constitution of the Federal Republic of Nigeria 1979.* Lagos, 1978.

Nigeria. Federal Ministry of Information. *Federal Republic of Nigeria National Policy on Education,* Lagos, 1977.

Nigeria. Federal Ministry of Information. *Reports of the Constitution Drafting Committee,* Lagos, 1976.

Nigeria. Kaduna State Government. *White Paper on the Report of the Mass Literacy Committee.* Kaduna, 1980.

Nigeria. Oyo State Government. *Primary School Syllabus of Oyo State.* Ibadan, (n.d.).

Nkrumah, Kwame. *Consciencism: Philosophy and Ideology for Decolonization.* New York: Monthly Review Press, 1970.

Ofari, Earl. *The Myth of Black Capitalism.* New York: Monthly Review Press, 1970.

Osoba, S.O. "The Nigerian Power' Elite, 1952-65: A Study in Some Problems of Modernisation." Paper presented at the Historical Society of Nigeria 16th Annual Congress: December, 1970. A condensed version of this paper appears in *African Social Studies*, edited by P.W.C. Gutkind and P. Waterman. London: Heinemann, 1977.

Oyewole, Anthony. "Toward a Language Policy For Nigeria." *Odu* 15 (July 1977) pp. 74-90.

Sarason, Seymour B. *The Culture of the School and the Problem of Change.* Boston: Allyn and Bacon Inc., 1971.